Cambridge Elements

Elements in Applied Evolutionary Science
edited by
David F. Bjorklund
Florida Atlantic University

IMPROVING BREASTFEEDING RATES

Evolutionary Anthropological Insights for Public Health

Emily H. Emmott
University College London

CAMBRIDGE
UNIVERSITY PRESS

Shaftesbury Road, Cambridge CB2 8EA, United Kingdom

One Liberty Plaza, 20th Floor, New York, NY 10006, USA

477 Williamstown Road, Port Melbourne, VIC 3207, Australia

314–321, 3rd Floor, Plot 3, Splendor Forum, Jasola District Centre,
New Delhi – 110025, India

103 Penang Road, #05–06/07, Visioncrest Commercial, Singapore 238467

Cambridge University Press is part of Cambridge University Press & Assessment,
a department of the University of Cambridge.

We share the University's mission to contribute to society through the pursuit of
education, learning and research at the highest international levels of excellence.

www.cambridge.org
Information on this title: www.cambridge.org/9781009217484

DOI: 10.1017/9781009217491

First published 2023

A catalogue record for this publication is available from the British Library.

ISBN 978-1-009-21748-4 Paperback
ISSN 2752-9428 (online)
ISSN 2752-941X (print)

Improving Breastfeeding Rates

Evolutionary Anthropological Insights for Public Health

Elements in Applied Evolutionary Science

DOI: 10.1017/9781009217491
First published online: February 2023

Emily H. Emmott
University College London
Author for correspondence: Emily H. Emmott, emily.emmott@ucl.ac.uk

Abstract: Breastfeeding is championed as an effective way to improve global health, associated with improved health outcomes for children and mothers. Various public health strategies to promote breastfeeding have been developed and implemented for over four decades, yet progress has stagnated, and exclusive breastfeeding rates remain low globally. From an *evolutionary anthropological perspective*, low breastfeeding rates seem like an 'evolutionary puzzle'; breastfeeding is a behaviour which confers survival and fitness advantage to children and mothers, yet so many mothers do not breastfeed exclusively or at all. *Is this a globally maladaptive behaviour?* Framing breastfeeding as a maternal investment behaviour, an evolutionary perspective directs us to consider the fitness costs of breastfeeding, together with the role of social learning and cultural norms. Indeed, an evolutionary anthropological perspective provides insights to why some breastfeeding-promotion strategies may have been ineffective, while pointing to potentially promising policies and practices which have been overlooked.

Keywords: breastfeeding, evolutionary anthropology, public health, infant feeding, mothering

ISBNs: 9781009217484 (PB), 9781009217491 (OC)
ISSNs: 2752-9428 (online), 2752-941X (print)

Contents

1 Introduction: Breastfeeding as a Public Health Issue

How do people feed their babies? This seems like a simple question to answer. As mammals, all human infants need milk. However, many parents and caregivers will know that infant feeding can be a complex process to navigate, with multiple decisions to be made: first, where options are available, babies can be fed at the breast or via a bottle. If bottle-feeding, the content is typically formula or pumped/expressed breastmilk. With this, babies can be exclusively breastfed, exclusively formula-fed, or in combination in varying amounts. Second, if the bottle is used, either with expressed breastmilk or formula, other caregivers can feed the baby (although, note, other women can and do breastfeed others' babies). Third, other liquids and foods can be introduced alongside breastmilk or formula. While it's uncommon for caregivers in higher-income countries to provide anything but breastmilk or formula to infants before four to six months, in many cultures, caregivers may introduce other things such as water and pureed/mashed foods (beikost) even earlier. When feeding a baby, therefore, one must consider *how* they are fed, *who* feeds them, and *what* they are fed. Consequently, feeding practices can be diverse within and between populations, as well as within individuals through time.

With so many factors to consider, parents and caregivers may wonder whether there is a 'best' way to feed a baby. Focusing on infant health and development, breastmilk is championed as the best form of nutrition for infants (Andreas et al., 2015; Ballard & Morrow, 2013), and the current World Health Organization (WHO) guidance recommends on-demand exclusive breastfeeding for the first six months, then in combination with solid food and other liquids for two years (WHO, 2018). This recommendation stems from mounting evidence which finds breastfeeding to be associated with a myriad of health and developmental benefits for children, including lower risks of infectious diseases and infant mortality (Binns et al., 2016; Duijts et al., 2009; Victora et al., 2016; WHO Collaborative Study Team, 2000), better neurological development and higher IQ (Binns et al., 2016; Fitzsimons & Vera-Hernández, 2022; Horta et al., 2015; Raju, 2011; Victora et al., 2016), and lower risks of later-life obesity and type 2 diabetes (Binns et al., 2016; Victora et al., 2016). This is perhaps unsurprising given the complexity of breastmilk, which contains key macro and micronutrients needed by young infants, as well as bioactive factors such as immunological and growth factors which promote health and optimal development (Andreas et al., 2015; Ballard & Morrow, 2013; Hinde & German, 2012). Breastmilk is also dynamic in nature, with its composition changing depending on infant/child age and need – including changes to its antibody, fat, and protein content (Andreas et al., 2015; Ferris et al., 1988; Hinde & German,

2012; Michaelsen et al., 1990). Consequently, breastmilk is near-impossible to replicate with breastmilk substitutes such as formula. Beyond breastmilk, the act of breastfeeding promotes closer contact between mother and child, which may confer independent benefits: skin-to-skin contact has been associated with better infant thermoregulation and lower stress reactivity (Cleveland et al., 2017), as well as better developmental outcomes for preterm infants (Almgren, 2018; Feldman et al., 2014; Norholt, 2020).

Breastfeeding has also been associated with multiple long-term benefits for mothers, including lower risks of breast cancer (Chowdhury et al., 2015; Collaborative Group on Hormonal Factors in Breast Cancer, 2002), ovarian cancer (Chowdhury et al., 2015), coronary heart disease (Tschiderer et al., 2022), type 2 diabetes (Chowdhury et al., 2015), and depression (Chowdhury et al., 2015; Dias & Figueiredo, 2015). For more immediate benefits, some studies have reported longer sleep durations for breastfeeding mothers (Gettler et al., 2022; Hughes et al., 2018; Srimoragot et al., 2022). This may counter common notions of breastfeeding, where breastfeeding is often perceived to cause greater sleep disturbances for mothers who must feed on-demand through the night (as evidenced, e.g., by the emergence of 'formula dream-feeds' where caregivers provide formula to otherwise-breastfed infants before going to bed to encourage overnight infant sleep). While studies *have* reported more night-wakings for older breastfed babies (Figueiredo et al., 2017), studies also suggest formula-feeding parents are more likely to overestimate infant sleep duration (Rudzik et al., 2018; Rudzik & Ball, 2021). While longer sleep for breastfeeding mothers has not been a consistent finding (e.g., see Doan et al., 2014; Rudzik et al., 2018; Rudzik & Ball, 2021), a recent systematic review suggests that, on average, breastfeeding mothers get around 30 minutes more sleep per night (Srimoragot et al., 2022). Physiologically, breastfeeding leads to oxytocin and prolactin release, which may facilitate maternal relaxation and sleep. For example, breastfeeding-induced oxytocin release has been associated with lower levels of cortisol, decreased blood pressure, reduced anxiety, and reduced stress (Uvnäs-Moberg et al., 2020). Breastfeeding women were also found to spend longer in 'deep sleep', associated with greater restoration and recovery (Doan et al., 2014). While the impact of breastfeeding on sleep duration and quality is likely moderated by various factors such as household situation and infant/child age, the physiological processes which promote relaxation and sleep may be particularly important for maternal well-being given the wide-ranging detrimental health consequences of sleep deprivation and prolonged stress (AlDabal & BaHammam, 2011), which is often present in the early postpartum period.

Given these benefits for mothers and children, encouraging breastfeeding has been on the global public health agenda for several decades (Lutter & Morrow, 2013), with the WHO setting a global exclusive breastfeeding target of 50 per cent by 2025 (WHO, 2014). However, global breastfeeding rates remain low, with only an estimated 43 per cent of infants exclusively breastfed for six months in 2015 (UNICEF, 2016). Exclusive breastfeeding rates are notably low in higher-income nations across the Global North (Victora et al., 2016), for example, with less than 25 per cent of infants estimated to be exclusively breastfed for six months in Europe (Theurich et al., 2019). Recent global estimates of the cost of 'not breastfeeding' points to around 823,000–600,000 annual excess child deaths, and around 20,000–10,000 annual excess maternal deaths from ovarian and breast cancer (Victora et al., 2016; Walters et al., 2019), with a total aggregated economic loss of US$341.3 billion (Walters et al., 2019). While these costs disproportionality fall on lower- and middle-income countries due to the greater morbidity and mortality risks in these contexts, higher-income countries are not fully protected: for example, in the United Kingdom, where breastfeeding rates are one of the lowest in the world, analysis of data from children born between 2000 and 2002 suggests that exclusive breastfeeding would have reduce infant hospitalisations by over 50 per cent for diarrhoea, and over 30 per cent for respiratory tract infections (Quigley et al., 2007). An improvement of UK breastfeeding rates to 45 per cent of mothers exclusively breastfeeding for four months is estimated to save more than £31 million (approx. US$35 million; Renfrew et al., 2012).

Overall, globally, current breastfeeding rates are lower than desired by public health bodies, leading to high levels of preventable morbidity and mortality among children and mothers. From an evolutionary perspective, this is puzzling (Sellen, 2007): why, if breastfeeding confers such clear survival benefits, are so many mothers not breastfeeding exclusively, breastfeeding for longer, or breast-feeding at all? *Is this a globally maladaptive behaviour?* In the pages to follow, I discuss the causes of low breastfeeding rates from a public health perspective and explore various policies, practices, and interventions which have been developed and implemented to improve breastfeeding. I then explore breast-feeding from an evolutionary anthropological perspective, and critically exam-ine what an evolutionary perspective may offer to current public health approaches. Evolutionary approaches to public health, or evolutionary public health in short, is an emerging field which guides research and knowledge-building through application of evolutionary theory such as natural selection and life history theory, along with the understanding of evolved, biologically normal health-related behaviours (Ball, 2017; Fewtrell et al., 2020; Wells et al., 2017). Through this Element, I outline how an evolutionary approach to breastfeeding behaviours and practices may provide new insights around promoting and supporting breastfeeding.

Before continuing, a few caveats: throughout this Element, I draw on my research expertise on the determinants of breastfeeding in the West, and in particular the United Kingdom and England, meaning many of the examples presented in the Element will be from this context. Thus, the examples outlined in the Element are by no means comprehensive. As importantly, there is currently a debate around using gender-neutral and inclusive language when discussing breastfeeding, in recognition that some people who are biologically female who do not identify as women give birth and breastfeed, and some people chest-feed (Spatz, 2020; Walks, 2017). While I fully recognise this argument, there is also a long history of erasing and excluding women in the field of health and medicine, and where the sex is hidden, the default tends to be 'male' (Criado-Perez, 2019; Dusenbery, 2018; Gribble et al., 2022) – meaning there is a continuing need to highlight and advocate for women's health specifically. Furthermore, while opinions differ, some have suggested that removal of sexed terms, relating specifically to the female sex, in effort to address issues around gender, can be counterproductive by conflating the two (Gribble et al., 2022). It is likely that the significance and impact of using gender-neutral/inclusive language regarding breastfeeding depend on the individual and community context, with both *pros* and *cons*. These complexities are reflected by different decisions taken by various organisations; for example, with La Leche League adopting gender-neutral/inclusive language throughout (Walks, 2017), while the British Pregnancy Advisory Service opting to maintain sexed language in general, with their strategy focusing on amending language on a case-by-case basis (BPAS, n.d.). After careful consideration, throughout this Element, I refer to 'breastfeeding' as a technical/clinical term in relation to lactation from breast tissue. By 'women' and 'mothers', I refer to a diverse group of people who are biologically female, which include those with varying gender identities.

2 Why Are Breastfeeding Rates so Low? A Public Health Perspective

2.1 Background: A Brief History of the Emergence of Infant Feeding as a Public Health Issue

In contemporary Western societies, breastfeeding is now commonly promoted as the 'best' way to feed a baby (Berry & Gribble, 2008; Jelliffe & Jelliffe, 1977). However, this is a relatively recent shift in discourse over the past fifty years. In the late nineteenth and early twentieth centuries, even before the availability of commercial formula, infants across the United States and Europe were commonly supplemented with some form of home-made breastmilk substitute, usually whole cow's milk with added carbohydrates and water, as well as cereal-based beikost (Fomon, 2001). This suggests that breastfeeding initiation rates were presumably high, but with combination feeding being the norm. Due to the lack of milk pasteurisation and safe storage, infant ingestion of cow's milk came with high risks of disease, ranging from botulism and hepatitis to typhoid, with the most common diseases being bovine tuberculosis and diarrhoea (Atkins, 2003). In the United Kingdom, for example, an estimated 500,000 infants lost their lives between 1850 and 1950 due to consuming milk from diseased cattle (Atkins, 2003).

As 'safer' commercial formulas became available, active advertisement of breastmilk substitutes became prevalent across the globe; and with limited understanding of breastmilk composition and the nutritional needs of infants, formula was initially advertised as 'just like mother's milk' and even endorsed by some medical professionals (Fomon, 2001; Jelliffe & Jelliffe, 1977; Joseph, 1981; Palmer, 2009). This was combined with the presumed insufficiency of breastmilk alone, including deficits in iron and vitamin D, as well as the risk of drug exposure through breastfeeding – which meant early beikost introduction remained common (Fomon, 1987). Unsurprisingly, breastfeeding initiation rates gradually declined through the twentieth century in Western countries, reaching its lowest levels in the 1970s in the United States (Fomon, 2001), and many infants received no breastmilk whatsoever.

The consequences of breastmilk substitute promotions were catastrophic for some communities. One famous case uncovered by Cicely Williams in the 1930s, in the formally British-occupied colonies of British Malaya (the Malay Peninsula and Singapore), was the notably high infant mortality caused by the direct promotion of sweetened condensed milk to postpartum mothers by Nestlé, with many mothers being told it was superior to breastmilk (Brady, 2012; Joseph, 1981). Not only were early breastmilk substitutes nutritionally inadequate, families were often not able to appropriately clean and sterilise bottles (Atkins, 2003), nor access clean water (Anttila-Hughes et al., 2018). In many cases, bottle feeding was actively harmful for infants (Palmer, 2009). Furthermore, due to the expenses associated with formula, caregivers could be tempted to dilute the milk ('formula stretching') – making it even more nutritionally inadequate for babies.

While the harm done by inappropriate breastmilk substitutes were recognised and reported as early as the 1930s, formula companies continued to promote their products across the globe (Palmer, 2009). Some of the promotion practices were highly problematic, particularly in lower- and middle-income countries.

This included distribution of free samples by women dressed up as nurses, and the claim that formula was easy and safe to use, despite lack of resources for many families to prepare the milk safely and accurately (Finkle, 1993). In one study, it was estimated that the availability of formula in lower- and middle-income countries led to an increase in infant mortality by 9.4 infants per 1,000 births (Anttila-Hughes et al., 2018). By the late 1960s, campaigners began to actively push against the promotion of formula, eventually leading to a widely read investigative book on formula, *The Baby Killer* (see Brady, 2012). This was followed by a worldwide boycott of Nestlé through the late 1970s and early 1980s. With wider recognition of infant deaths caused by inappropriate formula use, in 1979, WHO and the United Nations Children's Fund (UNICEF) convened an international meeting on the issue, which finally led to restrictions on formula advertising in many nations across the globe (Brady, 2012).

By the 1990s, the focus expanded from restricting formula advertising to include protecting, promoting, and supporting breastfeeding (Brady, 2012). This was kicked off by the Innocenti Declaration, formally agreed and endorsed by thirty-one countries and multiple global organisations including UNICEF, WHO, and World Bank, which called on governments to establish breastfeeding-promoting policies and practices, including the adoption of 'ten steps to success-ful breast-feeding' practices for maternity services (see *2.3 Strategies to improve breastfeeding*; UNICEF, 2006). In 2012, WHO set a global target of 50 per cent exclusive breastfeeding for six months by 2025 (Gupta et al., 2013; WHO, 2014). With these global policy directives breastfeeding rates improved, with an esti-mated increase of exclusive breastfeeding rates from 34 per cent to 41 per cent in lower- and middle-income countries between 1990 and 2004 (UNICEF, 2006). However, recent stagnation in breastfeeding rates have also been reported across the globe (Cai et al., 2012; Gupta et al., 2013; Matanda et al., 2014; Roberts et al., 2013; Waits et al., 2018). In the United Kingdom, for example, while breastfeeding initiation rates rose from 76 per cent in 2005 to 81 per cent in 2010, only 1 per cent of mothers reported exclusive breastfeeding at six months in 2010 (McAndrew et al., 2012). The most recent available government figures suggest that only 47.6 per cent of infants in England were being breastfed at all at six to eight weeks in 2020–1 (Office for Health Improvement and Disparities, 2021).

2.2 The Determinants of Breastfeeding from a Public Health Perspective

It is important to acknowledge that some women and infants are not able to breastfeed exclusively or at all due to medical or physiological reasons (Martin, 2017). For example, while very rare, some women have insufficient glandular tissue in the breast, meaning not enough breastmilk is produced (McGuire, 2019). Factors such as premature birth, high maternal stress, and obesity can delay the onset of milk production, which can lead to low milk supply (Martin, 2017). Tongue-tie, which is a relatively common congenital issue affecting an estimated 3–4 per cent of infants, can cause problems and discomfort with breastfeeding, and in some cases infants are not able to breastfeed sufficiently due to restricted tongue movements (Hall & Renfrew, 2005). However, it is argued that the majority of women and infants are physically able to breastfeed (Neifert, 2001). This means that the stubbornly low global breastfeeding rates seen today are unlikely to be a purely biological phenomenon, and the success of global, national, and local policies and practices around improving breast-feeding rates depend on addressing the various barriers to breastfeeding. So, why are breastfeeding rates so low?

To understand the determinants of health-related behaviours such as breast-feeding, contemporary public health approaches typically employ some form of socio-ecological model which recognises the importance of the wider 'extrasomatic' (i.e., beyond the body) environment as an influence on indi-viduals (Golden & Wendel, 2020; McLeroy et al., 1988). While various models have been proposed, they typically draw inspiration from Ecological Systems Theory (Bronfenbrenner, 1979, 1992), which is a widely used con-ceptual framework developed by Urie Bronfenbrenner in the 1970s to holis-tically understand the determinants of child development (McLeroy et al., 1988). Ecological Systems Theory categorises the extrasomatic environment into multiple levels around the individual (Figure 1): the *microsystem* reflects the immediate environment around the individual, such as the household, friends, and family, which may have direct influence on the individual. The *exosystem* captures the environment that does not directly interact with the individual but may have indirect impact, such as local government bodies, health and social care services, as well as friends-of-friends. The *mesosystem* captures the interaction between the *microsystem* and *exosystem*. The *macro-system* captures wider sociocultural beliefs and systems, such as norms and legislation, while the *chronosystem* captures the history and changes through time. Taking infant feeding as an example, the opinions and behaviours of immediate family can be placed into the microsystem, while wider advertising campaigns of formula can be placed into the exosystem. Of course, these two factors may interact, namely: the advertising campaign may influence the opinions and behaviours of immediate family – and this process can be placed into the mesosystem. The legislation around formula advertising can be placed into the macrosystem, and how all these factors change over time can be placed in the chronosystem.

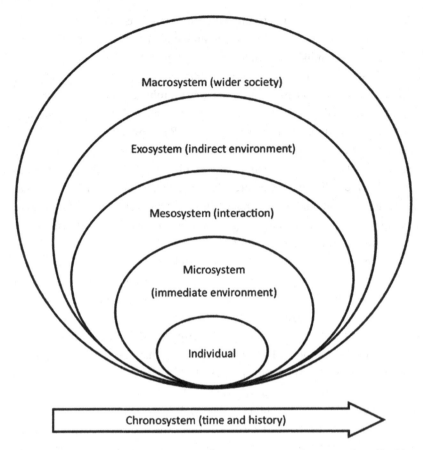

Figure 1 Visual representation of Ecological Systems Theory as described by
Bronfenbrenner (1979, 1992)

The consequences of the wider socio-ecology on health and health-related
behaviour is also often discussed in terms of the *social determinants of health*
(Marmot, 2005). In its essence, the social determinants of health reflects the
embodiment of the extrasomatic environment and its expression at the individual level, with particular focus on the inequity in health outcomes between
marginalised/disadvantaged and privileged groups based on factors such as
race, income, and education. Research consistently finds that those from disadvantaged social and economic circumstances have comparatively higher morbidity and mortality risks within and between nations (WHO, 2008). Similar
trends have been observed with breastfeeding in some (but not all; see Roberts
et al., 2013) contexts, particularly within higher-income populations. For
example, in the United States, non-Hispanic Black mothers and those with
lower levels of educational attainment are typically less likely to breastfeed

(Standish & Parker, 2022). In the United Kingdom, an analysis of six cohort studies spanning 1985–2010 found that younger mothers and those with lower levels of educational attainment were more likely to stop breastfeeding before six weeks, although mothers from minority ethnic backgrounds were more likely to continue breastfeeding (Simpson et al., 2022). Improving breastfeeding rates has been suggested as an effective tool to address the higher burden of disease among disadvantaged populations, as the biggest health benefits from breastfeeding are observed among lower-income groups and nations (Roberts et al., 2013).

Individual-Level Determinants of Breastfeeding

With this conceptual background, public health researchers have identified multiple and complex determinants of low breastfeeding rates. Starting at the individual level, the fundamental cause behind low levels of breastfeeding is often attributed to the lack of knowledge. For example, in higher-income populations where breastfeeding is often not the norm, perceived inadequacy in breastmilk supply is a common reason given by mothers causing early breastfeeding cessation (Galipeau et al., 2018; Gatti, 2008; Morrison et al., 2019; Noonan, 2011). However, in many cases, breastmilk supply is adequate (Noonan, 2011); rather, typical infant feeding practices and behaviours are incorrectly taken to be signals of excessive infant hunger. For example, mothers may be unaware that cluster-feeding, where newborns spend a prolonged time (often hours) feeding at the breast, is a normal feeding pattern and not a reflection of low supply (Noonan, 2011). Similarly, frequent night-waking is not necessarily a sign of inadequate milk supply; in fact, infants typically do not sleep through the night, and night-waking is thought to be an important mechanism to maintain breastmilk supply (Fu et al., 2021; Rudzik & Ball, 2021). However, the biologically normal high demand of milk by infants can be unexpected for many mothers, causing a lack of confidence with milk supply, leading them to introduce formula to 'fill up baby' (Galipeau et al., 2018; Gatti, 2008; Heinig et al., 2006; Noonan, 2011). At the same time, mothers may also be unaware that breastfeeding is not necessarily an easy task, just like pregnancy and birth – and that it is common across cultures for mothers to find aspects of breastfeeding challenging or difficult (Dharel et al., 2020; Myers et al., 2021; Page et al., 2022; Taylor et al., 2019). The lack of knowledge around breastfeeding challenges and the assumption that it is 'easy' may lead to a mismatch between expectation and reality, leaving some mothers to feel like they are 'failing' at breastfeeding (Burns et al., 2010; Larsen et al., 2008). Overall, with low maternal confidence in breastfeeding, many mothers begin to introduce formula milk (Gatti, 2008), which in turn risks actual low supply as breastmilk production is highly linked to the 'demand' of breastmilk.

Conversely, in lower- and middle-income populations where breastfeeding is generally more common, different gaps in infant feeding knowledge are thought to lead to the early introduction of solid foods and other liquids. For example, across many countries, including Ghana, Cote d'Ivoire, Brazil, Nepal, India, and Vietnam to name a few, it is common practice to give liquids such as tea, water, dairy, sugar water, or honey to newborns (Chang et al., 2021; Dharel et al., 2020; Ramani et al., 2019; Roberts et al., 2013). This is often thought to reflect the lack of knowledge that babies under six months old do not need any additional liquids, as breastmilk composition and volume changes depending on infant need (UNICEF, 2016). Furthermore, mothers may not be aware that providing other liquids/foods can lead to increased risks of infectious disease, and providing too much water to newborns can lead to issues such as water intoxication and weight loss (Nguyen et al., 2013; Williams, 2006). While recent research shows that breastfeeding is generally perceived to be good for infant health and development in many lower- and middle-income settings (Dharel et al., 2020; Ramani et al., 2019), early introduction of other foods and liquids may be seen as complementary rather than detrimental. Mothers may not perceive introduction of additional liquids as conflicting with exclusive breastfeeding practices (Ramani et al., 2019), particularly if breastfeeding is still on-demand and prolonged.

Microsystem-Level Determinants of Breastfeeding

Of course, the individual-level 'knowledge barriers' to breastfeeding are throughout to be driven by proximal and distal socio-ecological factors. Within the microsystem, partner and family attitudes, knowledge, and behaviour around infant feeding has consistently been found to influence maternal breastfeeding practices across populations (Abbass-Dick et al., 2019; Chang et al., 2021; Emmott et al., 2020a; Gharaei et al., 2020; Ramani et al., 2019). A recent systematic review of family members' views on breastfeeding suggests that, in many contexts, partners and grandmothers may not have up-to-date knowledge on breastfeeding and safe infant feeding practices, which in turn hinder maternal breastfeeding through ineffective or inappropriate support and advice (Chang et al., 2021). For example, one study from Northeastern Ethiopia reports a practice of delaying breastfeeding and discarding colostrum (the yellowy 'first milk' before mature breastmilk is produced) due to views that colostrum is 'dirty' and bad for the baby, with grandmothers being a common source of this knowledge (Legesse et al., 2015). However, colostrum is a highly nutritious and protective first food for infants, and breastfeeding as soon as possible after birth is associated with better breastfeeding outcomes (UNICEF, 2016). In another example from a study involving informal workers in India, participants reported that mothers-in-law encouraged early introduction of complementary foods such as buffalo milk to ensure babies do not become dependent on breastmilk, to ensure mothers can return to work without issue (Horwood et al., 2020). Among lower-income women in the United States, some mothers reported being pressured by family members to introduce formula, including some instances where family members went against the mothers' wishes by giving formula/beikost to the baby (Heinig et al., 2006). These example clearly show that, across different cultural contexts, family members can sometimes act as barriers to breastfeeding by asserting incorrect knowledge and pressurising mothers to stop breastfeeding.

However, studies also show how family and friends can be crucial sources of support for breastfeeding mothers. For example, when family members are involved in receiving breastfeeding education with the mother, thereby empowering the wider family with breastfeeding knowledge, mothers may feel more confident about breastfeeding and breastfeed for longer (Abbass-Dick et al., 2019; Gharaei et al., 2020). In the United Kingdom, mothers who breastfed for longer were much more likely to report an extensive support network around them (Emmott et al., 2020a), suggesting that a wide range of supporters around the mother may facilitate breastfeeding. Within the diverse range of potential supporters, partners may be particularly important for breastfeeding outcomes, with several studies from high- and middle-income countries finding that partner encouragement of breastfeeding is associated with longer breastfeeding duration (Ogbo et al., 2020).

Beyond family and friends, healthcare practitioners are also identified as key sources of breastfeeding information, advice, and support. A systematic review of randomised and quasi-randomised controlled trials has shown that breastfeeding support provided by healthcare professionals such as midwives are generally associated with improved breastfeeding outcomes across different populations (McFadden et al., 2017). However, as found with family and friends, information and support from healthcare workers do not *always* lead to a positive impact on breastfeeding practices: in one reported case in Lesotho, midwives actively recommended providing regular water to newborns, introducing a new feeding practice into the community which was not practiced by previous generations (Almroth et al., 2000) – highlighting that the effectiveness of 'official' advice and support is only ever going to be effective if the information is accurate. Similarly, in the United Kingdom, receiving breastfeeding information from health visitors (specially trained early-years public health nurses) was not a strong predictor of breastfeeding duration (Chambers et al., 2022), with some women reporting out-of-date and conflicting advice (Chambers et al., 2022; Emmott et al., 2020a).

Information and support from family, friends, and healthcare practitioners clearly matter for breastfeeding practices and outcomes, but the evidence above suggests the effects of support on breastfeeding may differ depending on the quality and characteristics of support. For example, perhaps counterintuitively, high paternal caregiving has been associated with shorter breastfeeding durations in the United Kingdom and Canada (Emmott & Mace, 2015; Myers et al., 2021; Rempel et al., 2017), suggesting that support with infant care may lead to less breastfeeding, not more. One key consideration is that the *provision of support* may be confounded by the *need for support*, and greater maternal support needs may reflect underlying issues and challenges with breastfeeding which could be causing the breastfeeding cessation (Myers et al., 2021; Page et al., 2022). Understanding the true effect of support on breastfeeding is therefore a complex undertaking.

To add to the complexity, the same support may impact mothers differently depending on the context. For example, one study from the United Kingdom found that the association between support and breastfeeding continuation varied depending on the type of breastfeeding problems experienced by the mother: when mothers experienced pain and discomfort with breastfeeding (such as blocked milk ducts), receiving 'helpful support' from family and friends was associated with breastfeeding for longer; whereas when mothers reported perceived insufficiency with their breast-milk, receiving 'helpful support' was associated with earlier breastfeeding cessation (Page et al., 2022). As perceived insufficiency with milk is generally associated with lower breastfeeding confidence (Galipeau et al., 2018; Gatti, 2008; Heinig et al., 2006; Noonan, 2011), this result may indicate that mothers who are confident with breastfeeding are better able to overcome breastfeeding problems with the support of family and friends, while those who lack confidence may rely on the support to stop breastfeeding. In Western contexts, studies suggest that support which is responsive, empathetic, and affirmational may encourage breastfeeding by enabling positive maternal self-evaluation, while one-directional provision of information and practical support without consideration of maternal needs may hinder breastfeeding, likely by undermining maternal confidence and autonomy (Davidson & Ollerton, 2020; McLeish et al., 2021). Overall, current studies on the impact of information and support on breastfeeding suggest context-dependent, complex causal pathways which require careful teasing apart.

Exosystem-Level Determinants of Breastfeeding

Beyond the mother's immediate environment, the exosystem and wider societal factors can influence breastfeeding through various pathways, with local institutions playing an important role. One interesting example comes from an analysis of mothers with lower levels of education within the UK Millennium Cohort Study, which found that infants born just before the weekend were less likely to be breastfed. This was hypothesised to be caused by the Monday–Friday work structure where mothers did not receive adequate infant feeding support at hospital over the weekend (Fitzsimons & Vera-Hernández, 2022). Similar 'weekend effects' have been found in terms of general increased risk of mortality (Chen et al., 2019), suggesting that local health systems and structures can indirectly influence maternal breastfeeding outcomes.

Another key type of institution frequently found to impact breastfeeding duration is workplaces and employers (Dinour & Szaro, 2017), which is perhaps unsurprising given that paid work generally conflicts with on-demand breastfeeding across populations. For successful continuation of breastfeeding, particularly for newborns and younger babies who require frequent feeds, mothers require flexible working arrangements to incorporate breastfeeding, or at the very least protected time and appropriate facilities to express and store breastmilk to maintain supply. Breastfeeding-supportive employer policies and practices, for example provision of lactation space and breaks, has been associated with longer breastfeeding durations across several high- and middle-income countries (Dinour & Szaro, 2017). Of course, maternal employment is often only possible with childcare, and where children are looked after away from the mother, policies and practices of childcare providers can also impact breastfeeding continuation. For example, in the United States, children who were looked after by paid childcare providers which allowed mothers to breastfeed on site and accommodated bottle-feeding with expressed breastmilk were breastfed for longer (Batan et al., 2013). Clearly, factors within the exosystem can underpin the practicalities of infant feeding for mothers, which may help or hinder mothers in meeting their breastfeeding goals and desires. Even when accurate information, knowledge, and support is readily available in the microsystem, structural barriers in the exosystem may mean mothers are unable to carry out optimal breastfeeding practices.

The exosystem is also a space where knowledge and norms around infant feeding is transmitted and spread through society, filtering through to the individual. As described under the brief history of infant feeding, this includes past advertisement campaigns for formula which have actively conveyed the incorrect and harmful message that formula milk is equivalent to or better than breastmilk. A study from the United States showed that contemporary formula advertisements and promotions, even without explicit messaging around its qualities in comparison to breastmilk, can cause confusion and doubts around breastfeeding (Parry et al., 2013), suggesting that passive information around infant feeding may still have strong influences on normative beliefs around breastfeeding. In contemporary Western populations, for example, the lack of breastfeeding portrayed on television, news, and magazines may create an impression that breastfeeding is an 'unusual' infant feeding behaviour. An unrealistic portrayal of infant feeding (e.g., calm, sleeping newborns who do not frequently feed) may create an impression that normal infant feeding cues and demands are a sign of excessive hunger, leading to worries that breastfeeding is inadequate. In Britain, a content analysis of television programmes and newspaper articles from 1999 highlighted that bottle-feeding was more commonly portrayed than breastfeeding (Henderson et al., 2000), with the representation that formula was the 'normal' way to feed infants. Furthermore, teenagers in Scotland reported that they had seen bottle-feeding on TV more frequently than breastfeeding (Swanson et al., 2006), highlighting that media portrayals of infant feeding are picked up by the general public. The other side of the coin is that mass media campaigns can also be an effective tool to normalise and promote breastfeeding. For example, in Vietnam, maternal exposure to TV adverts promoting exclusive and on-demand breastfeeding was associated with an increased likelihood of exclusive breastfeeding (Nguyen et al., 2017). Overall, the exosystem can pose a variety of practical barriers and constraints around breastfeeding, as well as impact maternal perceptions of normative infant feeding practices.

Macrosystem-Level Determinants of Breastfeeding

All the outlined determinants of breastfeeding at the individual, microsystem, and exosystem levels are ultimately influenced by the cultural norms, values, and legal structures in the macrosystem. For example, legislation to restrict and/or regulate formula advertisements can ensure only accurate information about formula is presented. In the United Kingdom, advertisements of 'breastmilk substitutes' and formula for infants under six months is banned, while in Australia, advertisements of formula for infants under twelve months is banned. Consequently, formula adverts in parenting magazines are less common in the United Kingdom and Australia compared to countries such as the United States and Canada, where no such legislations exist (Berry et al., 2012). However, the effectiveness of such legislations is not always clear: as profit-making companies, formula producers will inevitably seek ways to increase sales; and in the

United Kingdom and Australia, formula companies actively promote follow-on and toddler formula milks. While these do not directly target infants, studies suggest they are nonetheless perceived by parents and caregivers to be advertising infant formula (Berry et al., 2012; Brown et al., 2020). Formula companies also often position themselves as scientific experts in pregnancy and infant feeding, providing information and advice on websites, social media, and magazines (Brown et al., 2020; Gupta et al., 2013; Laurent, 2003; Pereira-Kotze et al., 2020). Some companies have even set up infant feeding and parenting helplines. This creates opportunities for formula companies to directly engage with parents and caregivers, evidencing that formula companies often find 'work-arounds' to the legal restrictions on formula advertisements.

Importantly, legislation is unlikely to be effective unless it is aligned with local cultural norms and attitudes. For example, in the United Kingdom, The Equality Act 2010 made it illegal for individuals and organisations to treat a woman unfavourably because she is breastfeeding. It is illegal to harass or discriminate against breastfeeding mothers, including requesting them to stop breastfeeding or cover up in public (Maternity Action, 2022). Nonetheless, women have reported feeling uncomfortable about breastfeeding openly in public, with worries about being judged (Boyer, 2012). Where breastfeeding is not the cultural norm, it can be perceived as an 'abnormal' behaviour, causing discomfort and evoking feelings of disgust (Boyer, 2012; Morris et al., 2016). Even in contexts where breastfeeding is common, taboos around breastfeeding openly in public may exist. For example, in India and South Africa where breastfeeding is comparatively more common, male workers expressed the expectation that women should not breastfeed in public, meaning working women had to employ strategies to continue breastfeeding in private or stop breastfeeding altogether (Horwood et al., 2020). Without tackling wider norms, legislations to promote and protect breastfeeding is unlikely to be effective.

2.3 Past Strategies to Improve Breastfeeding: Has It Worked?

As outlined above, the global public health focus on improving breastfeeding rates has led to a wealth of research on factors which hinder or support breastfeeding. Synthesising decades of evidence, low breastfeeding rates have broadly been attributed to gaps in breastfeeding-supportive policies at national and local levels, aggressive promotion of breastmilk substitutes, cultural norms and practices which hinder breastfeeding, and lack of skilled support from health professionals (Gupta et al., 2013). Improvements to breastfeeding rates and practices are therefore seen to be dependent on direct access to high-quality breastfeeding support from trained breastfeeding counsellors, limiting access to formula promotions, and positive cultural attitudes and norms regarding breast-feeding (Gupta et al., 2013; UNICEF, 2016; WHO, 2018).

In line with this, the WHO has recommended that countries should control marketing of formula and other breastmilk substitutes as well as 'engage in vigorous campaigns to promote breastfeeding' (WHO, 2014, p.12). To remove the harmful marketing of breastmilk substitutes, the World Health Assembly, comprised of WHO, UNICEF, and national-level health ministers and subject experts, recommends adherence to the International Code of Marketing of Breastmilk Substitutes, which calls for restrictions on health and nutrition claims for breastmilk substitutes and prohibition of promotions and gifting of breastmilk substitutes to the general public, mothers, and healthcare workers (Becker et al., 2022; WHO, 2017a). With specific focus on ensuring early breastfeeding initiation and exclusive breastfeeding, breastfeeding promotion and support through hospital and community health services have been identi-fied as key areas for intervention (UNICEF, 2006; UNICEF, 2016; WHO, 2017). The Baby-Friendly Hospital Initiative, launched by WHO and UNICEF, advocates for breastfeeding-friendly maternity services; and their flagship 'Ten Steps to Successful Breastfeeding' (Ten Steps) provides key guidance for hospitals and clinical practice, including ensuring staff have the knowledge and skills to support breastfeeding, facilitating skin-to-skin contact and breastfeeding as soon as possible after birth, and counselling mothers on the use and risks of bottles (Table 1; WHO & UNICEF, 2018). Recognising the need for antenatal and postnatal support, UNICEF and WHO also recommend breastfeeding counselling in the community as an effective public health inter-vention, focusing on providing breastfeeding information and empowering women to breastfeed (UNICEF, 2016; WHO, 2018). Overall, these global strategies informed by available evidence have influenced breastfeeding-related policies, practices, and interventions at national and local levels (Lutter & Morrow, 2013; UNICEF, 2006).

Evaluations of these global policies and strategies highlight some success, with a systematic review of fifty-eight research publications from nineteen countries finding that adherence to the Ten Steps is associated with greater levels of breastfeeding and exclusive breastfeeding practices (Pérez-Escamilla et al., 2016). In a randomised control trial in Belarus, mothers who gave birth in Ten Steps hospitals were much more likely to breastfeed exclusively and for longer, with 49.8 per cent of mothers continuing to breastfeed at six months in the Ten Steps intervention group compared to 36.1 per cent of the control group (Kramer et al., 2001). Furthermore, a Cochrane systematic review of seventy-three studies across twenty-nine countries on formal breastfeeding support found that, overall, support interventions were associated with longer

Table 1 Ten steps to successful breastfeeding, revised 2018 version (WHO & UNICEF, 2018)

Ten Steps to Successful Breastfeeding	
Critical Healthcare Management Procedures	
1. Hospital policies	a. Comply fully with the International Code of Marketing of Breast-Milk Substitutes and relevant World Health Assembly resolutions
	b. Have a written infant feeding policy that is routinely communicated to staff and parents
	c. Establish ongoing monitoring and data management systems
2. Staff competency	Ensure that staff have sufficient knowledge, competence, and skills to support breastfeeding
Key Clinical Practices	
3. Antenatal care	Discuss the importance and management of breastfeeding with pregnant women and their families
4. Care right after birth	Facilitate immediate and uninterrupted skin-to-skin contact and support mothers to initiate breastfeeding as soon as possible after birth
5. Supporting mothers with breastfeeding	Support mothers to initiate and maintain breastfeeding and manage common difficulties
6. Supplementing	Do not provide breastfed newborns any food or fluids other than breastmilk, unless medically indicated
7. Rooming-in	Enable mothers and their infants to remain together and to practise rooming-in 24 hours a day
8. Responsive feeding	Support mothers to recognise and respond to their infants' cues for feeding
9. Bottles, teats, and pacifiers	Counsel mothers on the use and risks of feeding bottles, teats, and pacifiers
10. Discharge	Coordinate discharge so that parents and their infants have timely access to ongoing support and care

breastfeeding durations as well as exclusive breastfeeding (McFadden et al., 2017). Indeed, the popularisation and implementation of WHO recommendations across the globe have coincided with an increased prevalence in exclusive breastfeeding from an estimated 33 per cent in 1995 to 39 per cent in 2010 (Cai et al., 2012).

However, despite over forty years of global policy to promote and improve breastfeeding, improvements in global breastfeeding rates have stagnated (Gupta et al., 2013). In part, this is attributed to the lack of adherence to the WHO guidelines at the national level (Gupta et al., 2013), as well as disregard of the International Code of Marketing of Breastmilk Substitutes by formula companies (Becker et al., 2022). However, the story may be more complex with differences between contexts: in England, for example, WHO and UNICEF guidance has been translated into national-level health policies and practice for decades (Chambers et al., 2022; Public Health England, 2021), mirrored by an increase in breastfeeding initiation rates from an estimated 66.2 per cent in 2005–6 to 73.7 per cent in 2010–1 (Nuffield Trust, 2022). Despite this, there have been minimum improvements since, with breastfeeding initiation rates hovering at around 74 per cent for the next ten years (Nuffield Trust, 2022). Breastfeeding continuation has also remained low, with only 45–48 per cent of mothers providing any breastmilk at six to eight weeks (Nuffield Trust, 2022). Investigations into the effectiveness of breastfeeding interventions in the United Kingdom show that most randomised control trials have been ineffective at increasing breastfeeding initiation or duration (Hoddinott et al., 2011; Jolly et al., 2012), while implementation of the Baby-Friendly Hospital Initiative has not been associated with improved breastfeeding duration, although it seemed to improve initiation rates (Fallon et al., 2019). This hints to issues beyond uptake of WHO recommendations, bringing into question the potential effectiveness of the current global strategy in breastfeeding. *What is going on?*

One approach which may provide some insight is an *evolutionary anthropological perspective*. An *evolutionary perspective* encourages application of evolutionary theory to understand contemporary behaviour and public health issues, while an *anthropological perspective* encourages the explicit consideration of behavioural variations across populations. Evolutionary public health, which incorporates an evolutionary anthropological perspective, is an emerging field which examines health and behaviour in relation to *inclusive fitness*, or the relative propensity for you and your relatives to pass on your genes to the next generation (Wells et al., 2017). Overall, this approach makes it explicit that humans do not always behave to maximise health, but may act to maximise reproduction. An evolutionary anthropological perspective also provides a useful framework in directing and organising knowledge around 'how' behaviours exist (understanding the causal pathways and mechanisms), and 'why' behaviours exist (understanding the current utility and adaptive function of the behaviour; i.e., how the behaviour impacts survival, reproduction, and inclusive fitness) (Emmott et al., 2021). Consideration of both mechanism and function can bring forward new insights, leading to a comprehensive understanding of breastfeeding behaviour, while alignment of research findings between mechanisms and functions promotes research validity.

3 Breastfeeding from an Evolutionary Anthropological Perspective

3.1 Breastfeeding as an Evolved Behaviour

From an evolutionary anthropological perspective, breastfeeding is an *evolved behaviour* shaped through forces such as natural selection. Lactation is one of the defining characteristic of mammals with a long and gradual evolutionary history, with a diverse range of lactation systems and strategies observed across species (Fewtrell et al., 2020; Hinde & German, 2012; Lefèvre et al., 2010; Sellen, 2007). Ultimately, lactation may have conferred a selective advantage in unpredictable and/or low-quality environments: the transfer of immunological, hormonal, and nutritional fluids from mother to offspring reduces short-term fluctuations in offspring food provision, as the mother can draw on their own energy and nutritional reserves (Fewtrell et al., 2020; Hinde & German, 2012). Furthermore, as milk is easier for juveniles to digest with minimal foraging cost, it is more energy efficient for offspring to receive milk than to access food in the environment; and lactation also allows offspring to inhabit environments which may be suitable for adults but less suitable for juveniles (Hinde & German, 2012). These factors in varying degrees likely led to greater offspring survival and improved maternal reproductive success.

In primates, including in humans, milk is comparatively dilute with high water but low fat and protein content. This type of milk composition is generally associated with frequent nursing and a comparatively long period of lactation (Hinde & German, 2012; Sellen, 2007). Interestingly, the human lactation system is notable in that it includes a relatively early introduction of complementary foods alongside breastmilk (i.e., mixed-feeding) unseen in other primates (Fewtrell et al., 2020; Martin, 2017; Sellen, 2007). While studies of infant physiology suggest that infants are optimally adapted for the introduction of complementary solids from around four to six months of age, as reviewed previously, early introduction of small amounts of foods and/or other liquids is common across populations (Martin, 2017; Sellen, 2007). In comparison, in both wild orangutans and chimpanzees, juveniles begin supplementing nursing with solids at around a year old (Lonsdorf et al., 2020; Smith et al., 2017). Early mixed-feeding among humans is not limited to contemporary populations, with bioarchaeological evidence from Archaic South American hunter-gatherers suggesting introduction of complementary foods soon after birth (Halcrow et al., 2017), while feeding vessels with traces of animal milk have been found in graves of infants from the Bronze and Iron Age period in Germany (Dunne et al., 2019). This suggests that, at the very least, early mixed-feeding has been practiced for thousands of years in varying socio-ecologies.

Interestingly, human milk also holds comparatively high levels of different oligosaccharides compared to other primates (Hinde & German, 2012), which may be related to early mixed-feeding combined with large-group living: oligosaccharides promote a healthy gut microbiome (Thomson et al., 2018), which is known to prevent and reduce gastrointestinal infections and diarrhoea (Picard et al., 2005). The risk of infectious disease is already higher with group living, and the risk of gastrointestinal infections increases with introduction of complementary foods and other liquids. With the vulnerability of infants to gastrointestinal infections and diarrhoea, there may have been a strong selection pressure to provide additional protection to infants against these diseases throughout the weaning period.

The comparatively early introduction of mixed-feeding in humans likely co-evolved with our unique cooperative childrearing system (Martin, 2017; Sellen, 2007), where successful reproduction and offspring survival is dependent on high levels of involvement and cooperation with kin and non-kin caregivers (i.e., allomothers) (Emmott & Page, 2019). The provision of complementary foods and liquids to infants and young children is one way allomothers can support mothers and their children. One important characteristic of cooperative childrearing in humans is its flexibility, in that who provides support and how they provide support to mothers and children varies widely between populations (Emmott & Page, 2019). This is also reflected in the variation of weaning practices across cultures, from when complementary foods and liquids are introduced to when breastfeeding ends (Sellen, 2007). Overall, then, early mixed-feeding seems to be an evolved biological norm in humans, although how this is expressed varies substantially between populations (Martin, 2017).

Understanding the evolutionary background to breastfeeding and breastmilk provides insights around typical and expected infant feeding behaviours in humans. First, humans evolved for high-frequency nursing, in line with the recommendation that on-demand breastfeeding is optimal for breastfeeding. Infant fussiness and frequent waking are to be expected, as infants evolved to demand frequent feeding (Fewtrell et al., 2020), and does not signal insufficient milk supply or poor quality milk. Second, like breastfeeding, mixed-feeding in humans is an evolved behaviour and a crucial aspect of infant feeding (Fewtrell et al., 2020; Martin, 2017; Sellen, 2007). The fact that infants are not solely dependent on breastmilk for a prolonged period allows for a high level of flexibility and variation in how infants are fed and by whom, potentially allowing mothers and families to adapt feeding practices depending on the socio-ecological pressures they face. While substantial evidence suggests exclusive breastfeeding for four to six months is optimal for infants, as I discuss in detail below, what is optimal for infants may conflict with what is optimal for mothers.

3.2 Breastfeeding from an Inclusive Fitness Perspective

While breastfeeding is an evolved behaviour, it is also a behaviour with a high degree of variation within and between populations. This brings opportunities to examine it from an inclusive fitness perspective using a human behavioural ecological framework. Under this framework, we assume all behaviours are associated with costs and benefits, and that individuals experience limits to time, energy, and resources (Borgerhoff Mulder & Schacht, 2012). This leads to trade-offs, because the same time/energy/resource costs you pay through one behaviour cannot be simultaneously used in another. For many types of observed behaviours, the balance of costs and benefits vary depending on individual and environmental characteristics; and, in general, we assume individuals adjust their behaviours to maximise their inclusive fitness (whereby the benefits over-ride the costs) – leading to behavioural variation.

Within a human behavioural ecological framework, breastfeeding is viewed as a costly maternal investment behaviour, transferring energy and other physiological resources from mother to child (Emmott & Page, 2019). Indeed, the subjective costs of breastfeeding has been reported cross-culturally, with many mothers describing aspects of breastfeeding as demanding and draining (Burns et al., 2010; Page et al., 2022). Energetically, exclusive breastfeeding is estimated to require around 450–700 kcal a day (Butte & King, 2005), and is of course a time-consuming activity due to the frequent nursing required by human infants. Breastfeeding is also associated with lactational amenorrhea, or temporary postpartum infertility, with clear reproductive costs (Stuebe & Chen, 2022). In wild chimpanzees, lactation has been associated with higher viral richness (indicating more infections), suggesting trade-offs between nursing and somatic maintenance (Negrey et al., 2022), and similar health costs may exist in humans.

Importantly, the time and energy mothers expend through breastfeeding cannot be invested into other things, such as investing in resource production, domestic work, or investing in other children – meaning breastfeeding is associated with high opportunity costs. Across populations, studies show nursing mothers tend to receive higher levels of allomaternal support via food provisioning, domestic work, and/or childcare (Hawkes et al., 1997; Quinlan

& Quinlan, 2008), reflecting the reduced capacity of mothers to carry out those activities. Among diverse groups of hunter-gatherers including the Hiwi, Aché, and the Hadza, food production by breastfeeding mothers was lower than non-breastfeeding mothers, suggesting behavioural trade-offs between foraging activities and nursing (Hawkes et al., 1997; Hurtado et al., 1992). The conflict between nursing and other activities are also evident in higher-income, post-industrialised contexts, with return to paid employment being a strong predictor of breastfeeding cessation (Batan et al., 2013). Overall, a human behavioural ecological framework makes it explicit that breastfeeding is not 'free'.

With breastfeeding being an 'expensive' maternal caregiving behaviour with high opportunity costs, how much mothers are willing to invest in children via nursing may be different to how much children want to be nursed, leading to mother–infant conflict (Tully & Ball, 2013). Given the health and developmental benefits of breastfeeding for babies, the optimal amount of breastfeeding for an infant is likely to be higher than for the mother, who must balance the benefits against the cost to maximise her own inclusive fitness. Qualitative studies reflect how some mothers are acutely aware of this mother–infant conflict, exemplified by the quotes below from India and the United Kingdom:

> *Some children drink breastmilk for a long time, then the mother is troubled. If the child drinks mother's milk for a longer time, the mother becomes thin and weak and the child becomes healthy/fat. If the child is weaned after a year, then it is better. It takes a toll on the mother. My child drank up to his 3rd year. I had to apply neem [bitter] leaves on my breasts to make him stop being so dependent on my milk.* A mother from India (Horwood et al., 2020, p. 7)

> *Please recognise that us mums are only human. We would love to focus only on our babies we really would. But sometimes our other children need attention, we need to go back to work or sometimes we have the audacity of putting our mental health first. Sometimes that means giving an occasional bottle of formula or stopping at four months old. Stop making us feel like we have failed when we have actually done a damn good job!* A mother from the United Kingdom (Brown, 2016, p. 106)

Of course, the trade-offs and opportunity costs surrounding breastfeeding is highly context dependent, influenced by both maternal and socio-ecological characteristics. For example, in lower- and middle-income countries with higher risks of infectious disease/infant mortality, the marginal benefit of breastfeeding to maternal inclusive fitness (via child survival) is likely to be larger than in higher-income contexts (Roberts et al., 2013), which may partly explain why breastfeeding rates tend to be lower in post-industrialised higher-income nations. Similarly, in contexts where day-to-day activities cannot be readily combined with breastfeeding, the opportunity costs of breastfeeding are likely to be proportionally higher. For instance, studies show that, in higher-income populations, mothers often stop breastfeeding when they return to work, while paid maternity leave is a positive predictor of breastfeeding duration (Navarro-Rosenblatt & Garmendia, 2018). This suggests that many mothers are unable to invest in breastfeeding and paid work at the same time.

In fact, the difficulty in combining on-demand nursing with various production and work activities is seen cross-culturally, and this conflict is thought to be one reason behind the evolution of pair bonding (i.e., long-term, stable reproductive partnerships) and cooperative childrearing in humans (Emmott & Page, 2019; Quinlan & Quinlan, 2008). The availability of allomothers and what support they provide is likely to be key in modifying the opportunity costs of breastfeeding (Emmott et al., 2020a; Emmott & Mace, 2015): in contexts where allomothers support mothers via resource provisioning and domestic tasks, we can hypothesise that mothers are better able to direct their focus on infant care. This then reduces the opportunity costs of breastfeeding, facilitating longer nursing durations (Emmott et al., 2020a; Emmott & Mace, 2015; Emmott & Page, 2019; Quinlan & Quinlan, 2008). In contrast, where allomothers provide support via direct care to infants (such as by feeding and looking after them), the opportunity costs of breastfeeding may be high as nursing mothers are unable to easily take advantage of such support without mother–infant separation. For example, in the United Kingdom, infant care and feeding by partners and grandmothers has been associated with shorter breastfeeding durations (Emmott et al., 2020a; Emmott & Mace, 2015; Myers et al., 2021). Similarly, in an analysis of data from fifty-eight non-industrialised societies, availability of childcare support from allomothers has been associated with shorter breastfeeding durations, although it should be noted that most infants in these societies are breastfed for two years or longer (Quinlan & Quinlan, 2008). Overall, a human behavioural ecological perspective highlights the importance of allomaternal support on breastfeeding, and that different forms of support may have different consequences for breastfeeding.

In summary, from a maternal perspective, the 'right amount of breastfeeding' for her inclusive fitness is influenced by a range of factors which impact the costs and benefits of nursing. A human behavioural ecological approach to breastfeeding shows that it is not always in the mother's best interests to maximise child health via breastfeeding, and that limiting breastfeeding can be an *adaptive* rather than a *maladaptive* behaviour. Optimal breastfeeding practices are likely to vary within and between populations depending on individual and socio-ecological contexts (Fewtrell et al., 2020), reflected in the diverse range of infant feeding and weaning practices seen across cultures. This perspective highlights that, without alleviating the costs of breastfeeding, educating mothers on the benefits of breastfeeding for children is unlikely to be particularly effective in increasing breastfeeding over the long term, because maternal behaviours depend on the costs and benefits to *maternal inclusive fitness*, not just child fitness. Indeed, studies across higher-income populations show that mothers perceive breastmilk to be beneficial for infants, yet many mothers introduce formula to address the day-to-day challenges they face (Burns et al., 2010; Heinig et al., 2006).

3.3 Breastfeeding from a Cultural Evolution Perspective

Dominant narratives of infant feeding in the West portray breastfeeding as 'natural', counter to 'artificial' formula milk and bottle-feeding (Larsen et al., 2008). This language is often seen in breastfeeding-promotion materials and public health campaigns, including by the WHO, who describe breastmilk as 'the natural first food for babies' (Martucci & Barnhill, 2018). At first, this may seem in line with an evolutionary perspective: after all, breastfeeding is an evolved behaviour which exists in nature. However, labelling breastfeeding as 'natural' often conveys meanings of instinct, which is incorrectly perceived as an automatic and easy behaviour (Brown, 2016; Larsen et al., 2008; Scott & Mostyn, 2003; Williamson et al., 2012). In reality, infant feeding, including breastfeeding, is a costly, multi-faceted, complex, and skilled behaviour. It involves different behavioural components such as how to hold and latch the baby, how often to feed the baby, and which infant signals should be met by feeding the baby. The complexity of breastfeeding as a behaviour means it is difficult for mothers to figure out on their own, and mothers must rely on learning from others (Fewtrell et al., 2020; Wells, 2006).

Infant feeding as a predominantly socially learned behaviour brings opportunities to examine breastfeeding practices from a cultural evolution perspective (see Creanza et al., 2017). Within this perspective, we conceptualise breastfeeding as a learned behaviour where breastfeeding knowledge and practices are 'transmitted' between individuals. Transmission is not always perfect due to errors and changes individuals introduce, leading to variation in breastfeeding practices. Different forms of infant feeding practices 'compete' with each other to be transmitted; and over time, this leads to changes in normative infant feeding practices at the population level – or the *cultural evolution of infant feeding practices*. From this perspective, infant feeding is a complex behaviour built on what to feed, how to feed, and who feeds. Different feeding practices such as formula feeding, combination feeding, and exclusive breastfeeding can be viewed as cultural variants within a range of infant feeding practices. Therefore, mothers with infants have many choices to make: which infant feeding behaviours should they learn and take up? With infant feeding directly relating to infant health and survival, getting infant feeding 'wrong' can be costly for maternal inclusive fitness. *How can mothers increase their chance that they are learning the 'best' infant feeding practices?*

Because it is not possible to try out different infant feeding behaviours all at once (i.e., you cannot formula feed and exclusively breastfeed at the same time, or feed on demand and on schedule at the same time), and in most cases you don't immediately observe the inclusive fitness consequence of different infant feeding behaviours, mothers must gamble on whom to learn from. From an evolutionary perspective, we expect natural selection to have favoured individuals who were able to identify and preferentially learn from those who were most likely to practice the 'best' behaviour or have the 'best' knowledge, leading to the evolution of various social learning strategies and psychological mechanisms (Henrich & Gil-White, 2001; Rendell et al., 2011). For example, at the population level, the frequency of certain infant feeding behaviours (i.e., how common the behaviour is) can influence social learning through *conformity bias* (Morgan & Laland, 2012), where mothers may be more likely to take up the most popular infant feeding behaviours: if most people in your environment are feeding infants in a particular way, and they are generally alive and well, it seems reasonable to assume that this popular infant feeding behaviour is adaptive.

Interestingly, studies suggest that individuals may be more likely to conform to the majority behaviour when they are uncertain about the best behaviour (Morgan & Laland, 2012). This may partly explain why, as mentioned previously, low breastfeeding confidence and worries about supply is a strong determinant of early breastfeeding cessation in higher-income populations (Galipeau et al., 2018; Gatti, 2008; Heinig et al., 2006; Noonan, 2011): when mothers are unsure about infant feeding and experience feelings of doubt, they may default to the most common behaviour, which is to formula feed. In contrast, a strong belief that breastfeeding is the best infant feeding practice may facilitate going against the formula-feeding norm. In one study from Glasgow, for example, one mother described how her conviction that breastfeeding was the best thing for her infant gave her the determination to carry on, despite strong social pressures to bottle feed:

> *Nobody else in my family had ever breastfed. . . . My husband's mother was very negative about it. . . . Everybody is saying to you, 'Give up and get a bottle'. You feel everyone is watching you thinking how are you going to do. You are trying to latch on in tears because it is very painful with cracked nipples. You feel as if you are letting yourself down if you do not do it because you are determined to do it, and you feel that if you were to give up, everybody*

would say, 'Told you it was much better to give the bottle'. I think a lot of people do not realize how difficult it is to breastfeed. Even with some of my friends, I was only 22, said 'Oh my goodness you fed outside'. If I was going to visit them they did not want me to breastfeed in front of them. But I felt it was the best thing to do and I did not want to stop and give up just because so many people were being negative towards you. A mother from Glasgow (Scott & Mostyn, 2003, p. 273)

Mothers may also decide to preferentially learn from certain types of individuals, and a wide range of learning biases have been identified (Rendell et al., 2011). For example, studies have shown that people may be biased towards learning from 'familiar' individuals who are more like them (Healy, 2009), as well as people they know (Corriveau & Harris, 2009), compared to those who are unfamiliar. People are also more likely to preferentially learn from those who are perceived to be knowledgeable and successful regarding the behaviour (Henrich & Broesch, 2011), as well as those who are perceived to be successful, popular, and prestigious in general (Henrich & Gil-White, 2001). This means mothers may pick up infant feeding practices from a range of sources, such as from 'familiar' friends, 'knowledgeable' healthcare practitioners, 'experienced' mothers, and 'popular' celebrities and influencers. Indeed, as reviewed earlier, the extent to which other people influence maternal infant feeding practices are well-evidenced within the public health literature. For example, in one study from the United States, Spanish-speaking low-income women talked about strictly following infant feeding practices recommended by their 'knowledgeable' paediatrician (Heinig et al., 2006), while in a study from Glasgow, women mentioned how having a 'familiar' friend who breastfed made them feel like they could also breastfeed, with examples of mothers giving each other breastfeeding advice and tips (Scott & Mostyn, 2003). Adolescent mothers from England also expressed a preference for learning from other mothers who were currently breastfeeding, who were both 'familiar' and 'experienced' (Dykes et al., 2003).

Understanding the existence of different social learning strategies can help us identify specific types of individuals who may be highly influential in transmitting maternal infant feeding practices. Notably, maternal grandmothers are likely to be both 'familiar' and 'experienced' as well as 'knowledgeable', meeting multiple characteristics known to attract social learning. Maternal grandmothers may therefore be key sources of infant feeding knowledge; and indeed, maternal grandmothers are cross-culturally identified as particularly important sources of information and support for mothers. For example, among the Himba, which is a pastoralist population from Namibia, grandmothers were described to be key sources of breastfeeding information, support, and skill transfer, helping mothers overcome breastfeeding challenges. As one mother stated, '*My mom showed me how to put the baby to my breast. She told me to sit, not lie down [to feed]. She told me to feed him four times during the night*' (Scelza & Hinde, 2019, p. 384). Similarly, among adolescent mothers in England, maternal grandmothers were mentioned as valued sources of support and information, with one mother stating, '*My Mum gave me verbal comments and guided me*' (Dykes et al., 2003, p. 397). However, in higher-income populations with a historic 'crash' in breastfeeding due to a high uptake of formula feeding, many grandmothers today likely lack the experience and knowledge around breastfeeding – meaning mothers in these populations have lost key sources of infant feeding knowledge. In the United Kingdom, for example, mothers were more likely to self-report that they received breastfeeding information from their midwives (81.5 per cent) than grandmothers (41.7 per cent) (Emmott et al., 2020a). This may offer some explanation towards the persistent low exclusive breastfeeding rates despite increasing breastfeeding initiation rates in these populations contexts: many mothers may start breastfeeding with knowledge that it is 'good for the baby', but do not have easy access to others who hold breastfeeding skill.

It is important to note that active teaching and conscious learning via imitation is only one mechanism behind social learning (Rendell et al., 2011). The prerequisite of social learning is simply that there is a demonstrator of the behaviour along with an observer, and under various learning mechanisms, simply being exposed to nursing may encourage breastfeeding. For example, through 'observational conditioning', observing breastfeeding may facilitate social learning by creating an association between infants/young children and the breast. Through 'response facilitation', observing breastfeeding of a crying infant may facilitate social learning by signalling the context in which breastfeeding happens (i.e., feed infant when crying). In both examples, learning happens without active promotion or teaching of breastfeeding. The consequence is that simply providing more opportunities for girls and women to encounter breastfeeding may lead to an increase in breastfeeding rates.

At the same time, this may also explain why breastfeeding rates remain notably low in Western populations: in the West, children are typically viewed as vulnerable and innocent, requiring a safe, developmentally appropriate environment (Robinson, 2013). This inevitably leads to the segregation of children's lives from adult lives (Robinson, 2013), unintentionally situating breastfeeding as a conflicting activity which involves both infants/children and adults. The consequence is that breastfeeding is not readily incorporated into adult life. There are fewer opportunities for breastfeeding to exist in public, and fewer opportunities for others to socially learn about breastfeeding. In the

United Kingdom, for example, studies commonly find that parents rarely encounter anyone breastfeeding before having a baby, meaning women typically have limited opportunities for social learning before giving birth (Hoddinott & Pill, 1999; Scott & Mostyn, 2003).

A cultural evolution perspective also reveals how potentially harmful and maladaptive infant feeding practices can spread and be sustained in a population (Franz & Matthews, 2010; Morgan & Laland, 2012). The individual fitness consequences of various infant feeding practices are difficult to assess accurately, as the detrimental effects on infants may be delayed and/or not observed consistently, with potentially small marginal effects on infant survival and health. With no immediate observable harms and high levels of uncertainty about its consequences, incorrect advice and information is likely to persist, and mothers may end up preferentially learning maladaptive infant feeding behaviours. For example, as raised earlier in this Element, grandmothers have been found to 'transmit' suboptimal breastfeeding practices, including discarding colostrum combined with the incorrect belief that colostrum is dirty and bad for the baby (Legesse et al., 2015). The very fact that most people in the community are feeding infants in a certain way may reassure mothers that it is a 'good' or 'safe' behaviour to copy, encouraging conformity, which may explain why it has been particularly challenging to reduce pervasive behaviours such as early introduction of non-breastmilk across populations. The implication is that, given the importance of wider social information, changing infant feeding behaviours of individual mothers will likely require addressing infant feeding beliefs and knowledge of the community and those around the mother.

Overall, a cultural evolution perspective to breastfeeding provides a strong theoretical framework in understanding the transmission – or learning – of infant feeding knowledge and practice. With known learning biases such as conformity and familiarity, it explains why suboptimal or even harmful infant feeding behaviours may persist within populations despite decades of public health campaigns. Importantly, a cultural evolution perspective reiterates the importance of infant feeding knowledge across maternal social networks and the wider community: individuals perceived as familiar, experienced, knowledgeable, and/or popular by mothers may be important sources of social learning, meaning these key sources of information must hold good knowledge and information on infant feeding to ensure the transmission of 'best practice'. Furthermore, the visibility of breastfeeding, whether in public or private, may be an important opportunity for social learning; and where breastfeeding is not easily observed or the norm, helping mothers feel confident and certain about breastfeeding may weaken the transmission of formula feeding.

4 Can Evolutionary Anthropology Help Improve Breastfeeding Rates?

An evolutionary anthropological approach frames breastfeeding as a costly maternal caregiving behaviour, and mothers are assumed to weigh the costs and benefits to pursue their optimal behaviour which will vary by circumstance. Therefore, deviating from WHO's current breastfeeding recommendations may be an *adaptive* rather than a *maladaptive* behaviour. Furthermore, where the costs and benefits of various infant feeding practices are not immediately clear, such as with early introduction of other solids and liquids or scheduled versus on-demand feeding, social learning and cultural transmission may be important mechanisms explaining deviation from WHO recommendations. To increase breastfeeding rates and safer infant feeding practices, one must address the costs of breastfeeding together with improving knowledge of infant feeding across society.

These key arguments stemming from an evolutionary anthropological approach is clearly complementary to a general public health approach, and in line with previous findings such as the higher rates of breastfeeding in lower-income populations (due to greater marginal gains in child health from breast-feeding) (Roberts et al., 2013), lower rates of breastfeeding among mothers who return to work (due to increased opportunity costs of breastfeeding) (Batan et al., 2013; Dinour & Szaro, 2017), and the importance of friends, family, and healthcare professionals in supporting maternal breastfeeding (due to transmission of breastfeeding skill and knowledge, as well as instilling breastfeeding confidence) (Abbass-Dick et al., 2019; Chang et al., 2021; Davidson & Ollerton, 2020; Emmott et al., 2020a; Gharaei et al., 2020; McLeish et al., 2021; Ramani et al., 2019). However, the key strength of an evolutionary approach is that it provides a strong, unifying theoretical framework to understand behavioural variation between individuals and across socio-ecological contexts. With this, it has potential to highlight factors which are foundationally important in influencing breastfeeding rates and practices, allowing for a deeper understanding of cause and effect. Given the stagnation of global breastfeeding rates despite decades of public health effort, and with WHO's global breast-feeding target of 50 per cent exclusive breastfeeding by 2025, this may be a crucial point in history to re-examine what could be improved with current breastfeeding policies and practice.

Broadly, current strategies to improve breastfeeding rates focus on creating breastfeeding-friendly maternity and newborn services to promote and encourage breastfeeding (WHO & UNICEF, 2018); transmission of breastfeeding information and knowledge from breastfeeding counsellors (typically trained healthcare professionals or peer supporters) to the mother (WHO, 2018); and limiting advertisement of inappropriate foods for infants and young children, including formula (WHO, 2017a). For example, the United Kingdom's Baby-Friendly Initiative website states, '*We respond to the particular barriers [mothers] face by supporting health professionals to provide sensitive and effective care so that mothers can make an informed choice about feeding, get breastfeeding off to a good start and overcome any challenges. . . . In addition, we advocate for better regulation of marketing of breastmilk substitutes so that health professionals and families can receive scientific, unbiased and factual information about infant feeding*' (UNICEF UK, 2022a). From an evolutionary perspective, an immediate reflection is that these strategies focus almost solely on knowledge transfer, primarily to the mother, and do not address the wider costs of breastfeeding. While the importance of support is acknowledged, the support provided to mothers tends to be informational support, overlooking other types of support, such as practical and instrumental support, which alter the costs and benefits of breastfeeding (Emmott et al., 2020a; Emmott & Mace, 2015).

Focusing on knowledge transfer to mothers alone may increase the desire for mothers to breastfeed, leading to greater levels of breastfeeding initiation, but mothers may struggle to keep it up over time. Indeed, this pattern has been observed in England, where breastfeeding initiation rates have increased but exclusive breastfeeding rates remain low with only 45–48 per cent of mothers providing any breastmilk at six to eight weeks (Nuffield Trust, 2022). An evolutionary anthropological perspective highlights potential gaps in current strategies, helping us hypothesise what additional policies and practices may be effective in increasing breastfeeding rates and safer infant feeding practices. Next, I outline three evolutionarily informed potential opportunity areas for future breastfeeding strategies: to centre on the mother; to facilitate, not just promote; and to build the village.

Centre on the Mother: Breastfeeding Is Not Just About Child Health

Current WHO breastfeeding guidelines primarily exist to maximise child health and survival, with the 'best practice' for breastfeeding based on what is optimal for the child. This may explain why breastfeeding messages tend to centre on the benefits for children, as reflected in the promotional video by UNICEF UK, which states that breastfeeding 'supports loving relationships and brain development, and protects against cancer, obesity, diabetes, infections and sudden infant death syndrome' (UNICEF UK, 2017) – benefits which primarily relate to the child, not the mother. In fact, this focus on children rather than the mother is made explicit by UNICEF UK, which states, '*The Baby Friendly Initiative enables mothers to receive [help] within healthcare services, delivering a holistic, child-rights based pathway for improving care. We provide the crucial impetus that busy health professionals need to raise standards, enabling them to prioritise what is best for each and every child*' (UNICEF UK, 2022b).

However, from an evolutionary perspective, breastfeeding is one form of maternal investment behaviour amongst many, underpinned by mother–infant conflict. An evolutionary approach makes explicit that mothers do not necessarily behave to maximise individual child health. Rather, we predict mothers will be more likely to breastfeed, and breastfeed for longer, if it brings benefits to *them*, not just to their children – and communicating the potential benefits of breastfeeding for mothers may encourage breastfeeding. While the health benefits of breastfeeding for mothers are sometimes communicated, such as reduced risk of certain cancers and diabetes (Chowdhury et al., 2015), in reality, the marginal health gains for mothers via breastfeeding are arguably small and only recouped in the distant future. Thus, focusing on health benefits for mothers may not be particularly effective at incentivising breastfeeding. Instead, framing breastfeeding as a maternal investment behaviour naturally expands the focus of breastfeeding benefits beyond health, bringing to attention many potential day-to-day benefits which may make life 'easier' for mothers, such as quicker infant soothing (Quigley et al., 2017), quicker establishment of the circadian rhythm in infants (i.e., more sleep at night over day; Kikuchi et al., 2020), less preparation time compared to bottle-feeding, and fewer things to pack and carry when out and about. In short, centring on the benefits of breastfeeding for mothers and providing this information alongside the health benefits to children may amplify the perceived benefit of breastfeeding, leading to greater levels of breastfeeding.

Centring on the mother also means acknowledging the costs of breastfeeding. With the current breastfeeding policy and practice focusing on children, it primarily frames breastfeeding as a beneficial act – but both theory and evidence point to the high costs that accompany breastfeeding (Burns et al., 2010; Emmott et al., 2020a; Emmott & Mace, 2015; Page et al., 2022; Tully & Ball, 2013). Past policymakers may have worried that revealing the costs of breastfeeding may reduce maternal incentives to breastfeed, as reflected in healthcare guidance which have recommended withholding information on the challenges of breastfeeding (Emmott et al., 2020b). However, given the fact that most women experience problems and challenges when breastfeeding (Page et al., 2022; Scelza & Hinde, 2019), promoting a realistic expectation of breastfeeding better equips mothers to tackle these challenges, providing protection against the sense of failure and low breastfeeding confidence (Emmott et al., 2020b; Hoddinott & Pill, 1999). With the hypothesised and known importance of maternal confidence for breastfeeding continuation, particularly in contexts where breastfeeding is not the norm, honest information about both the costs and benefits of breastfeeding may lead to increased levels of breastfeeding. In fact, in the United Kingdom, the ineffectiveness of solely promoting the benefits of breastfeeding is increasingly acknowledged, recognising the 'mistake of imagining that our internationally low breastfeeding rates can be improved simply by educating about the benefits of breastfeeding more vigorously' (Trickey & Ashmore, 2017, p. 26).

Overall, an evolutionary anthropological approach reminds us that breastfeeding is a *maternal behaviour*. Framing breastfeeding around child health while ignoring the mother may not be an effective strategy, and may lead to unintended negative consequences such as fuelling a mismatch between breastfeeding expectations and reality. The child-centric approach to breastfeeding in public health has been a choice, perhaps reflecting the Western notions of children as vulnerable, which justifies paternalistic interventions and practices to protect children from harm (Robinson, 2013). It also coincides with the Western notions of motherhood that expects self-sacrifice and intensive parenting, which dismisses the costs of motherhood far beyond breastfeeding (Budds, 2021; Lowe, 2016). The medicalisation of breastfeeding (Taylor et al., 2019) pushes the narrative of breastfeeding towards health; yet an evolutionary anthropological approach clarifies that breastfeeding is better conceptualised as a costly maternal caregiving behaviour than a health behaviour. Going forward, future policy and practice may benefit from putting the mother at the centre, acknowledging both the costs and benefits of breastfeeding – rather than the current approach which inevitably reduces mothers to intervention targets 'to get to child health' (Emmott et al., 2021).

Facilitate, Not Just Promote: Tackle the Costs of Breastfeeding

To repeat, the current breastfeeding guidelines and strategies primarily focus on transferring breastfeeding knowledge and skill to individual mothers, with the global strategy focusing on 'promoting breastfeeding' (WHO & UNICEF, 2018; WHO, 2017b). However, as reviewed previously, a wide range of socio-ecological factors are recognised as important determinants of breastfeeding, with explicit acknowledgement that breastfeeding should not be viewed as an individual responsibility (UNICEF UK, 2022b). Despite this, most public health efforts to improve breastfeeding rates have been shy to address distal socio-ecological factors. Where distal factors are addressed, they focus on breastfeeding promotion in healthcare settings (WHO, 2017b) and limiting formula advertisements (WHO, 2017a). While important, these factors do not directly address the day-to-day costs and benefits of breastfeeding.

An evolutionary anthropological approach makes explicit that, without lowering the costs of breastfeeding, mothers are unlikely to breastfeed or to breastfeed for longer, regardless of how much knowledge and skill they have. In fact, breastfeeding in high-cost contexts could even be a *maladaptive* behaviour, harming maternal inclusive fitness, raising questions around the ethics of promoting breastfeeding without addressing the costs in such settings. By viewing breastfeeding as a costly maternal caregiving behaviour which conflicts with many activities, and acknowledging that childrearing in humans is a collective behaviour involving multiple parties, an evolutionary approach points to the importance of domains such as production/work and social support as key areas in addressing the costs of breastfeeding.

For example, given the high levels of conflict between maternal employment and breastfeeding, in contexts where maternal paid employment is common or necessary, many mothers would require six months of paid maternity leave or income support if they were to meet the WHO recommendation of six months exclusive breastfeeding. Indeed, studies have shown that the length of maternity leave correlates with breastfeeding duration across countries (Navarro-Rosenblatt & Garmendia, 2018); and simply educating women on the benefits of breastfeeding without addressing this structural barrier is unlikely to be effective. Similarly, availability of childcare for older children ensures mothers can invest more time and energy into breastfeeding their youngest. In one UK study, one mother described how the lack of childcare due to the COVID-19 pandemic ultimately led to her stopping breastfeeding earlier than she wanted to, highlighting the conflict between breastfeeding and wider childcare: '... *the guilt I felt because I got breastmilk into my oldest for five or six months ... the guilt I felt because I wasn't able to give [the youngest] the same thing. There's no question that if my oldest had been in nursery, I would have been able to breastfeed for longer, and I feel terrible about that'* (Emmott et al., 2022, p. 10). Again, telling women to breastfeed without ensuring provision of adequate childcare for those with multiple children is unlikely to facilitate breastfeeding.

Clearly, there are structural factors beyond the individual which impact the opportunity costs of breastfeeding. The consideration of the wider structural issues which impede breastfeeding have been repeatedly called for, yet change has been slow. The reasons behind this are hard to pinpoint, but it may partly stem from the assumption that the key barriers to breastfeeding are knowledge- and culture-related, leading to the underestimation of the socio-ecological factors that impact breastfeeding. Furthermore, breastfeeding policies tend to come under the domain of 'health', with limited powers to address wider structural or economic issues.

However, one area of opportunity within the domain of health is to engage with family members: evolutionary theory suggests that family members could increase or decrease the costs of breastfeeding depending on the types of support they provide (Emmott et al., 2020a; Emmott & Mace, 2015), and evidence supports the importance of kin support for breastfeeding, particularly from fathers and grandmothers (Abbass-Dick et al., 2019; Chang et al., 2021; Emmott & Mace, 2015). Yet, breastfeeding promotion and interventions rarely target anyone but the mother. Explaining and providing guidance to family members on how to support breastfeeding, such as offer to do household chores rather than hold the baby, may prove effective. Indeed, studies suggest that including fathers/partners and grandmothers within breastfeeding interventions may be more successful at improving breastfeeding outcomes (Abbass-Dick et al., 2019; Gharaei et al., 2020), perhaps because family members are better at providing the types of practical support which make it easier for mothers to breastfeed.

Overall, an evolutionary anthropological approach clarifies that breastfeeding promotion alone is unlikely to be effective in improving breastfeeding durations, and the costs of breastfeeding must be addressed to facilitate breastfeeding. The costs of breastfeeding are highly dependent on socio-ecological factors around the mother, such as situations with work, childcare, and wider family support. Given many of these factors are often beyond the control of individual women and mothers, public health bodies have a crucial role in addressing them and advocating for change.

Build the 'Village': Beyond One-to-One Breastfeeding Counselling

Studies have shown that provision of breastfeeding knowledge and skill from breastfeeding counsellors, often referred to as 'breastfeeding support', is generally associated with better breastfeeding outcomes (McFadden et al., 2017; WHO, 2018). The WHO recommends that all pregnant women and mothers with infants receive breastfeeding counselling by skilled individuals, either lay persons or healthcare professionals, who have been specifically trained to provide information and guidance on breastfeeding, help troubleshoot any issues, and potentially provide emotional support (WHO, 2018). From an evolutionary perspective, the effectiveness of this strategy is in line with findings that individuals are more likely to learn from those who are perceived as knowledgeable. Furthermore, skilled individuals such as healthcare professionals may be conferred prestige, further increasing the propensity for individuals to learn from them (Henrich & Gil-White, 2001).

However, an evolutionary perspective also highlights that limiting the source of breastfeeding support to trained breastfeeding counsellors may lead to missed opportunities and possible challenges. As breastfeeding counsellors are usually unknown to the mother, to promote social learning, breastfeeding counsellors must be framed as 'breastfeeding experts' to signal knowledge. However, this relies on mothers to trust the breastfeeding counsellors as experts; and where there is suspicion, the advice and information may be dismissed. Under hypothesised mechanisms of prestige bias, for example, if the individual who is the source of information is not respected, it hinders social learning and information transmission (Henrich & Gil-White, 2001). While not directly comparable, studies have shown that trust in experts is associated with the propensity for individuals to take recommended public health actions relating to COVID-19 mitigation (Ahluwalia et al., 2021), and the lack of trust towards experts was associated with low vaccine uptake (Jamison et al., 2019) – suggesting that framing breastfeeding counsellors as experts may backfire in some contexts. Furthermore, the professionalisation of breastfeeding counselling risks invalidating existing sources of knowledge in the community, which may inadvertently limit the sources of knowledge – as seen in the lower reliance on grandmothers for breastfeeding information in the United Kingdom (Emmott et al., 2020b). In short, if breastfeeding counsellors are not readily available to provide support, mothers may be left without anyone to learn from.

To ensure breastfeeding support is as effective as possible, it may be important to explicitly acknowledge that humans evolved a cooperative childrearing system. As reflected in the well-known proverb, 'it takes a village to raise a child', it also takes a village to breastfeed. In addition to one-to-one support by breastfeeding counsellors, tapping into this 'village' through a family and community-centred approach may have the potential to facilitate maternal breastfeeding even further. Indeed, studies consistently show that friends and family are important sources of childrearing and infant feeding knowledge across cultures; but the knowledge and support they provide are not always conducive in facilitating breastfeeding (Chang et al., 2021; Emmott et al., 2020b; Emmott & Mace, 2015; Horwood et al., 2020). Ensuring those around the mother are able to support her effectively, through informational, practical, or emotional support, may lead to improved breastfeeding rates and practices (Emmott et al., 2020b).

Of course, not all mothers have access to an extensive support network, and this may be particularly true in higher-income populations with nuclear family norms, as childrearing responsibilities tend to fall on individual caregivers, particularly the mother (Sear, 2021). In these contexts, actively building a network of supporters around the mother could lead to better outcomes. In Scotland, for example, mothers from one study said they preferred group breastfeeding counselling sessions over one-to-one support, as they were able to see others breastfeed, and felt a sense of familiarity with other participants who were also breastfeeding (Hoddinott et al., 2006). These, interestingly, are factors hypothesised to promote social learning.

5 Conclusion

Breastfeeding is championed as one of the most effective (and cost-effective) ways to improve global health, associated with improved survival, health, and development of children, as well as better maternal health. Decades of public health research on the determinants of breastfeeding has informed current strategies to improve breastfeeding rates and practices across nations. To date, global strategies to improve breastfeeding has primarily focused on breastfeeding promotion and knowledge transfer to the mother. While there has been some success, 'progress' in global breastfeeding rates has recently stagnated. It goes without saying that infant feeding mode is a choice, and dictating or forcing infant feeding practices are never acceptable. However, across populations, many mothers want to promote their children's health and development. For example, in the United Kingdom, where the benefits of breastfeeding for children are well-acknowledged, many women initiate breastfeeding but quit before they want to, meaning they are not able to meet their infant feeding goals (Emmott et al., 2020a). This has been associated with detrimental consequences for maternal well-being, including a strong sense of failure and guilt (Emmott et al., 2020a). Helping mothers breastfeed, if that is what they want, should be prioritised (which, to clarify, does not equate to removing or withholding support for those who choose to feed in different ways), and a critical re-examination of current breastfeeding strategies is arguably required.

Bringing an evolutionary anthropological perspective to breastfeeding, a review of current breastfeeding strategies and practices suggest three potential areas of opportunity: to centre on the mother (rather than child health); to facilitate, not just promote (by tackling the costs of breastfeeding); and to build the village (beyond one-to-one breastfeeding counselling). These three recommendations are of course in line with existing public health evidence on the determinants of breastfeeding, and are not revolutionary or new. This, understandably, may lead readers to question whether an evolutionary anthropological approach is particularly useful for public health. However, the challenge of the standard public health approach, often implicitly underpinned by ecological systems theory, is that so many factors are identified as potential determinants of breastfeeding, and it is often unclear which factors should be prioritised when developing breastfeeding strategies, practices, and interventions. The core strength of an evolutionary anthropological approach – and evolutionary public health – is the unifying theoretical foundation which helps identify key areas which may be particularly important in breastfeeding behaviour, among many possibilities.

To date, current breastfeeding strategies have focused on promoting child health while disregarding maternal well-being (Emmott et al., 2021). However, an evolutionary anthropological approach clarifies that breastfeeding is an evolved, skilled, and costly maternal investment behaviour with implications for maternal inclusive fitness, and it should be treated as such. This means acknowledging how breastfeeding impacts the mother, not just her infant. While intensive mothering norms situate mothers as primarily responsible for their children's well-being (Budds, 2021; Emmott et al., 2021), an evolutionary anthropological approach clarifies that breastfeeding is a behaviour influenced by multiple socio-ecological factors. Promotion of a single, rigid guideline is therefore unlikely to work for many mothers, not because mothers don't understand the benefits of breastfeeding or how to breastfeed, but because it doesn't work for their particular situation (Fewtrell et al., 2020; Martin, 2017). Indeed, recent criticisms of the standard public health approach include the 'focus on individual behaviors . . . but to ignore the drivers of these behaviors – the causes of the causes' (Marmot & Allen, 2014, p. S517). To improve breastfeeding rates and practices, then, focus should extend beyond knowledge transfer to mothers, with greater consideration of how we can create a wider environment that facilitates breastfeeding. As demonstrated in this Element, evolutionary approaches to public health points to areas for future research which may be productive in developing effective policies and practice.

References

Abbass-Dick, J., Brown, H. K., Jackson, K. T., Rempel, L., & Dennis, C.-L. (2019). Perinatal breastfeeding interventions including fathers/partners: A systematic review of the literature. *Midwifery, 75*, 41–51. https://doi.org/10.1016/j.midw.2019.04.001.

Ahluwalia, S. C., Edelen, M. O., Qureshi, N., & Etchegaray, J. M. (2021). Trust in experts, not trust in national leadership, leads to greater uptake of recommended actions during the COVID-19 pandemic. *Risk, Hazards & Crisis in Public Policy, 12*(3), 283–302. https://doi.org/10.1002/rhc3.12219

AlDabal, L., & BaHammam, A. S. (2011). Metabolic, endocrine, and immune consequences of sleep deprivation. *The Open Respiratory Medicine Journal, 5*, 31. https://doi.org/10.2174/1874306401105010031.

Almgren, M. (2018). Benefits of skin-to-skin contact during the neonatal period: Governed by epigenetic mechanisms? *Genes & Diseases, 5*(1), 24–6. https://doi.org/10.1016/j.gendis.2018.01.004

Almroth, S., Mohale, M., & Latham, M. (2000). Unnecessary water supplementation for babies: Grandmothers blame clinics. *Acta Paediatrica, 89*(12), 1408–13. https://doi.org/10.1080/080352500456552.

Andreas, N. J., Kampmann, B., & Mehring Le-Doare, K. (2015). Human breast milk: A review on its composition and bioactivity. *Special Issue: Neonatal Update 2015, 91*(11), 629–35. https://doi.org/10.1016/j.earlhumdev.2015.08.013.

Anttila-Hughes, J. K., Fernald, L. C., Gertler, P. J., Krause, P., & Wydick, B. (2018). Mortality from Nestlé's marketing of infant formula in low and middle-income countries. *National Bureau of Economic Research Working Paper Series, 24452*. https://doi.org/10.3386/w24452.

Atkins, P. J. (2003). Mother's milk and infant death in Britain, circa 1900-1940. *Anthropology of Food, 2*. https://doi.org/10.4000/aof.310.

Ball, H. L. (2017). Evolution-informed maternal–infant health. *Nature Ecology & Evolution, 1*(3), 73. https://doi.org/10.1038/s41559-017-0073.

Ballard, O., & Morrow, A. L. (2013). Human milk composition: Nutrients and bioactive factors. *Breastfeeding Updates for the Pediatrician, 60*(1), 49–74. https://doi.org/10.1016/j.pcl.2012.10.002.

Batan, M., Li, R., & Scanlon, K. (2013). Association of child care providers breastfeeding support with breastfeeding duration at 6 months. *Maternal and Child Health Journal, 17*(4), 708–13. https://doi.org/10.1007/s10995-012-1050-7.

Becker, G. E., Zambrano, P., Ching, C. et al. (2022). Global evidence of persistent violations of the international code of marketing of breast-milk substitutes: A systematic scoping review. *Maternal & Child Nutrition, 18* (S3), e13335. https://doi.org/10.1111/mcn.13335.

Berry, N. J., & Gribble, K. D. (2008). Breast is no longer best: Promoting normal infant feeding. *Maternal & Child Nutrition, 4*(1), 74–9. https://doi .org/10.1111/j.1740-8709.2007.00100.x.

Berry, N. J., Jones, S. C., & Iverson, D. (2012). Circumventing the WHO code? An observational study. *Archives of Disease in Childhood, 97*(4), 320. https:// doi.org/10.1136/adc.2010.202051.

Binns, C., Lee, M., & Low, W. Y. (2016). The long-term public health benefits of breastfeeding. *Asia Pacific Journal of Public Health, 28*(1), 7–14. https:// doi.org/10.1177/1010539515624964.

Borgerhoff Mulder, M., & Schacht, R. (2012). Human behavioural ecology. In *eLS*. John Wiley & Sons. https://doi.org/10.1002/9780470015902 .a0003671.pub2.

Boyer, K. (2012). Affect, corporeality and the limits of belonging: Breastfeeding in public in the contemporary UK. *Health & Place, 18*(3), 552–60. https://doi.org/10.1016/j.healthplace.2012.01.010.

BPAS (n.d.). *Trans, Non-binary and Intersex People.* British Pregnancy Advisory Service. Retrieved November 11, 2020, from www.bpas.org/ abortion-care/considering-abortion/trans-non-binary-and-intersex-people/.

Brady, J. P. (2012). Marketing breast milk substitutes: Problems and perils throughout the world. *Archives of Disease in Childhood, 97*(6), 529. https:// doi.org/10.1136/archdischild-2011-301299.

Bronfenbrenner, U. (1979). *The ecology of human development: Experiments by nature and design.* Harvard University Press.

Bronfenbrenner, U. (1992). *Ecological systems theory.* Jessica Kingsley.

Brown, A. (2016). What do women really want? Lessons for breastfeeding promotion and education. *Breastfeeding Medicine, 11*(3), 102–10. https://doi .org/10.1089/bfm.2015.0175.

Brown, A., Jones, S., & Evans, E. (2020). *Marketing of infant milk in the UK: what do parents see and believe.* First Steps Nutrition Trust. *https://static1.square space.com/static/59f75004f09ca48694070f3b/t/6053645514d0f3072adec94e/ 1616077909798/Marketing_of_infant_milk_in_the_UK-what_do_parents_ see_and_believe_finala.pdf.*

Budds, K. (2021). Validating social support and prioritizing maternal wellbeing: Beyond intensive mothering and maternal responsibility. *Philosophical Transactions of the Royal Society B, 376*(1827), 20200029. https://doi.org/10 .1098/rstb.2020.0029.

Burns, E., Schmied, V., Sheehan, A., & Fenwick, J. (2010). A meta-ethnographic synthesis of women's experience of breastfeeding. *Maternal & Child Nutrition*, *6*(3), 201–19. https://doi.org/10.1111/j.1740-8709.2009.00209.x.

Butte, N. F., & King, J. C. (2005). Energy requirements during pregnancy and lactation. *Public Health Nutrition*, *8*(7a),1010–27. https://doi.org/10.1079/PHN2005793.

Cai, X., Wardlaw, T., & Brown, D. W. (2012). Global trends in exclusive breastfeeding. *International Breastfeeding Journal*, *7*(1), 12. https://doi.org/10.1186/1746-4358-7-12.

Chambers, A., Myers, S., Emmott, E. H., & Page, A. E. (2022). *Emotional and informational social support from health visitors and breastfeeding outcomes in the UK*. https://doi.org/10.31219/osf.io/37cke.

Chang, Y.-S., Li, K. M. C., Li, K. Y. C. et al. (2021). Relatively speaking? Partners' and family members' views and experiences of supporting breastfeeding: A systematic review of qualitative evidence. *Philosophical Transactions of the Royal Society B: Biological Sciences*, *376*(1827), 20200033. https://doi.org/10.1098/rstb.2020.0033.

Chen, Y.-F., Armoiry, X., Higenbottam, C. et al. (2019). Magnitude and modifiers of the weekend effect in hospital admissions: A systematic review and meta-analysis. *BMJ Open*, *9*(6), e025764. https://doi.org/10.1136/bmjopen-2018-025764.

Chowdhury, R., Sinha, B., Sankar, M. J. et al. (2015). Breastfeeding and maternal health outcomes: A systematic review and meta-analysis. *Acta Paediatrica*, *104*(S467), 96–113. https://doi.org/10.1111/apa.13102.

Cleveland, L., Hill, C. M., Pulse, W. S. et al. (2017). Systematic review of skin-to-skin care for full-term, healthy newborns. *Journal of Obstetric, Gynecologic & Neonatal Nursing*, *46*(6), 857–69. https://doi.org/10.1016/j.jogn.2017.08.005.

Collaborative Group on Hormonal Factors in Breast Cancer. (2002). Breast cancer and breastfeeding: Collaborative reanalysis of individual data from 47 epidemiological studies in 30 countries, including 50 302 women with breast cancer and 96 973 women without the disease. *The Lancet*, *360*(9328), 187–95. https://doi.org/10.1016/S0140-6736(02)09454-0.

Corriveau, K., & Harris, P. L. (2009). Choosing your informant: Weighing familiarity and recent accuracy. *Developmental Science*, *12*(3), 426–37. https://doi.org/10.1111/j.1467-7687.2008.00792.x.

Creanza, N., Kolodny, O., & Feldman, M. W. (2017). Cultural evolutionary theory: How culture evolves and why it matters. *Proceedings of the National*

Academy of Sciences, *114*(30), 7782–9. https://doi.org/10.1073/pnas
.1620732114.

Criado-Perez, C. (2019). *Invisible women: Exposing data bias in a world designed for men*. Chatto & Windus.

Davidson, E. L., & Ollerton, R. L. (2020). Partner behaviours improving breastfeeding outcomes: An integrative review. *Women and Birth*, *33*(1), e15–e23. https://doi.org/10.1016/j.wombi.2019.05.010.

Dharel, D., Dhungana, R., Basnet, S. et al. (2020). Breastfeeding practices within the first six months of age in mid-western and eastern regions of Nepal: A health facility-based cross-sectional study. *BMC Pregnancy and Childbirth*, *20*(1), 59. https://doi.org/10.1186/s12884-020-2754-0.

Dias, C. C., & Figueiredo, B. (2015). Breastfeeding and depression: A systematic review of the literature. *Journal of Affective Disorders*, *171*, 142–54. https://doi.org/10.1016/j.jad.2014.09.022.

Dinour, L. M., & Szaro, J. M. (2017). Employer-based programs to support breastfeeding among working mothers: A systematic review. *Breastfeeding Medicine*, *12*(3), 131–41. https://doi.org/10.1089/bfm.2016.0182.

Doan, T., Gay, C. L., Kennedy, H. P., Newman, J., & Lee, K. A. (2014). Nighttime breastfeeding behavior is associated with more nocturnal sleep among first-time mothers at one month postpartum. *Journal of Clinical Sleep Medicine*, *10*(3), 313–9. https://doi.org/10.5664/jcsm.3538.

Duijts, L., Ramadhani, M. K., & Moll, H. A. (2009). Breastfeeding protects against infectious diseases during infancy in industrialized countries: A systematic review. *Maternal & Child Nutrition*, *5*(3), 199–210. https://doi
.org/10.1111/j.1740-8709.2008.00176.x.

Dunne, J., Rebay-Salisbury, K., Salisbury, R. B. et al. (2019). Milk of ruminants in ceramic baby bottles from prehistoric child graves. *Nature*, *574*(7777), 246–8. https://doi.org/10.1038/s41586-019-1572-x.

Dusenbery, M. (2018). *Doing harm: The truth about how bad medicine and lazy science leave women dismissed, misdiagnosed, and sick* (1st ed.). HarperOne, an imprint of HarperCollins.

Dykes, F., Moran, V. H., Burt, S., & Edwards, J. (2003). Adolescent mothers and breastfeeding: Experiences and support needs – An exploratory study. *Journal of Human Lactation*, *19*(4), 391–401. https://doi.org/10.1177/0890334403257562.

Emmott, E. H., Gilliland, A., Narasimhan, A. L., & Myers, S. (2022). Coping with 'lockdown Babies': Understanding postpartum maternal experience in London, UK. *OSF Preprints*. https://doi.org/10.31219/osf
.io/r7enw.

Emmott, E. H., & Mace, R. (2015). Practical support from fathers and grand-mothers is associated with lower levels of breastfeeding in the UK millennium cohort study. *PLOS ONE*, *10*(7), e0133547. https://doi.org/10.1371/journal.pone.0133547.

Emmott, E. H., Myers, S., & Page, A. E. (2021). Who cares for women with children? Crossing the bridge between disciplines. *Philosophical Transactions of the Royal Society B: Biological Sciences*, *376*(1827), 20200019. https://doi.org/10.1098/rstb.2020.0019.

Emmott, E. H., & Page, A. E. (2019). Alloparenting. In T. K. Shackelford & V. A. Weekes-Shackelford (Eds.), *Encyclopedia of Evolutionary Psychological Science* (pp. 1–14). Springer. https://doi.org/10.1007/978-3-319-16999-6_2253-1.

Emmott, E. H., Page, A. E., & Myers, S. (2020a). Typologies of postnatal support and breastfeeding at two months in the UK. *Social Science & Medicine*, *246*, 112791. https://doi.org/10.1016/j.socscimed.2020.112791.

Emmott, E. H., Page, A. E., & Myers, S. (2020b). Typologies of postnatal support and breastfeeding at two months in the UK: Response to comments by Harpur & Haddon. *Social Science & Medicine*, *252*, 112944. https://doi.org/10.1016/j.socscimed.2020.112944.

Fallon, V. M., Harrold, J. A., & Chisholm, A. (2019). The impact of the UK baby friendly initiative on maternal and infant health outcomes: A mixed-methods systematic review. *Maternal & Child Nutrition*, *15*(3), e12778. https://doi.org/10.1111/mcn.12778.

Feldman, R., Rosenthal, Z., & Eidelman, A. I. (2014). Maternal-preterm skin-to-skin contact enhances child physiologic organization and cognitive control across the first 10 years of life. *Temperament: Genetic and Environmental Factors*, *75*(1), 56–64. https://doi.org/10.1016/j.biopsych.2013.08.012.

Ferris, A. M., Dotts, M. A., Clark, R. M., Ezrin, M., & Jensen, R. G. (1988). Macronutrients in human milk at 2, 12, and 16 weeks postpartum1. *Journal of the American Dietetic Association*, *88*(6), 694–7. https://doi.org/10.1016/S0002-8223(21)02037-X.

Fewtrell, M. S., Mohd Shukri, N. H., & Wells, J. C. K. (2020). 'Optimising' breastfeeding: What can we learn from evolutionary, comparative and anthropological aspects of lactation? *BMC Medicine*, *18*(1), 4. https://doi.org/10.1186/s12916-019-1473-8.

Figueiredo, B., Dias, C. C., Pinto, T. M., & Field, T. (2017). Exclusive breast-feeding at three months and infant sleep-wake behaviors at two weeks, three and six months. *Infant Behavior and Development*, *49*, 62–9. https://doi.org/10.1016/j.infbeh.2017.06.006.

Finkle, C. L. (1993). Nestle, infant formula, and excuses: The regulation of commercial advertising in developing nations. *Northwestern Journal of International Law & Business.*, *14*, 602.

Fitzsimons, E., & Vera-Hernández, M. (2022). Breastfeeding and child development. *American Economic Journal: Applied Economics*, *14*(3), 329–66. https://doi.org/10.1257/app.20180385.

Fomon, S. J. (1987). Reflections on infant feeding in the 1970s and 1980s. *The American Journal of Clinical Nutrition*, *46*(1), 171–82. https://doi.org/10.1093/ajcn/46.1.171.

Fomon, S. J. (2001). Infant feeding in the 20th century: Formula and beikost. *The Journal of Nutrition*, *131*(2), 409S-20S. https://doi.org/10.1093/jn/131.2.409S.

Franz, M., & Matthews, L. J. (2010). Social enhancement can create adaptive, arbitrary and maladaptive cultural traditions. *Proceedings of the Royal Society B: Biological Sciences*, *277*(1698), 3363–72. https://doi.org/10.1098/rspb.2010.0705.

Fu, X., Lovell, A. L., Braakhuis, A. J., Mithen, R. F., & Wall, C. R. (2021). Type of milk feeding and introduction to complementary foods in relation to infant sleep: A systematic review. *Nutrients*, *13*(11). https://doi.org/10.3390/nu13114105.

Galipeau, R., Baillot, A., Trottier, A., & Lemire, L. (2018). Effectiveness of interventions on breastfeeding self-efficacy and perceived insufficient milk supply: A systematic review and meta-analysis. *Maternal & Child Nutrition*, *14*(3), e12607. https://doi.org/10.1111/mcn.12607.

Gatti, L. (2008). Maternal perceptions of insufficient milk supply in breastfeeding. *Journal of Nursing Scholarship*, *40*(4), 355–63. https://doi.org/10.1111/j.1547-5069.2008.00234.x.

Gettler, L. T., Samson, D. R., Kilius, E. et al. (2022). Links between household and family social dynamics with sleep profiles among BaYaka foragers of the Congo Basin. *Social Science & Medicine*, *311*, 115345. https://doi.org/10.1016/j.socscimed.2022.115345.

Gharaei, T., Amiri-Farahani, L., Haghani, S., & Hasanpoor-Azghady, S. B. (2020). The effect of breastfeeding education with grandmothers' attendance on breastfeeding self-efficacy and infant feeding pattern in Iranian primiparous women: A quasi-experimental pilot study. *International Breastfeeding Journal*, *15*(1), 84. https://doi.org/10.1186/s13006-020-00325-5.

Golden, T. L., & Wendel, M. L. (2020). Public health's next step in advancing equity: Re-evaluating epistemological assumptions to move social determinants from theory to practice. *Frontiers in Public Health*, *8*. www.frontiersin.org/articles/10.3389/fpubh.2020.00131.

Gribble, K. D., Bewley, S., Bartick, M. C. et al. (2022). Effective communication about pregnancy, birth, lactation, breastfeeding and newborn care: The importance of sexed language. *Frontiers in Global Women's Health, 3.* www .frontiersin.org/articles/10.3389/fgwh.2022.818856.

Gupta, A., Dadhich, J. P., & Suri, S. (2013). How can global rates of exclusive breastfeeding for the first 6 months be enhanced? *Infant, Child, & Adolescent Nutrition, 5*(3), 133–40. https://doi.org/10.1177/1941406413480389.

Halcrow, S. E., King, C. L., Millard, A. R. et al. (2017). Out of the mouth of babes and sucklings: Breastfeeding and weaning in the past. In C. Tomori, A. E. L. Palmquist, E. A. Quinn (Eds.), *Breastfeeding: New Anthropological Approaches* (pp.155–69). Routledge

Hall, D. M. B., & Renfrew, M. J. (2005). Tongue tie. *Archives of Disease in Childhood, 90*(12), 1211. https://doi.org/10.1136/adc.2005.077065.

Hawkes, K., O'Connell, J. F., & Blurton Jones, N. G. (1997). Hadza women's time allocation, offspring provisioning, and the evolution of long postmeno-pausal life spans. *Current Anthropology, 38*(4), 551–77. JSTOR. https://doi .org/10.1086/204646.

Healy, A. (2009). How effectively do people learn from a variety of different opinions? *Experimental Economics, 12*(4), 386–416. http://dx.doi.org/10 .1007/s10683-009-9220-1.

Heinig, M. J., Follett, J. R., Ishii, K. D. et al. (2006). Barriers to compliance with infant-feeding recommendations among low-income women. *Journal of Human Lactation, 22*(1), 27–38. https://doi.org/10.1177/0890334405284333.

Henderson, L., Kitzinger, J., & Green, J. (2000). Representing infant feeding: Content analysis of British media portrayals of bottle feeding and breast feeding. *BMJ, 321*(7270), 1196. https://doi.org/10.1136/bmj.321.7270.1196.

Henrich, J., & Broesch, J. (2011). On the nature of cultural transmission networks: Evidence from Fijian villages for adaptive learning biases. *Philosophical Transactions of the Royal Society B: Biological Sciences, 366*(1567), 1139–48. https://doi.org/10.1098/rstb.2010.0323.

Henrich, J., & Gil-White, F. J. (2001). The evolution of prestige: Freely conferred deference as a mechanism for enhancing the benefits of cultural transmission. *Evolution and Human Behavior, 22*(3), 165–96. https://doi.org/10.1016/S1090-5138(00)00071-4.

Hinde, K., & German, J. B. (2012). Food in an evolutionary context: Insights from mother's milk. *Journal of the Science of Food and Agriculture, 92*(11), 2219–23. https://doi.org/10.1002/jsfa.5720.

Hoddinott, P., Chalmers, M., & Pill, R. (2006). One-to-one or group-based peer support for breastfeeding? Women's perceptions of a breastfeeding peer coach-ing intervention. *Birth, 33*(2), 139–46. https://doi.org/10.1111/j.0730-7659 .2006.00092.x.

Hoddinott, P., & Pill, R. (1999). Nobody actually tells you: A study of infant feeding. *British Journal of Midwifery, 7*(9), 558–65. https://doi.org/10.12968/bjom.1999.7.9.8264.

Hoddinott, P., Seyara, R., & Marais, D. (2011). Global evidence synthesis and UK idiosyncrasy: Why have recent UK trials had no significant effects on breast-feeding rates? *Maternal & Child Nutrition, 7*(3), 221–7. https://doi.org/10.1111/j.1740-8709.2011.00336.x.

Horta, B. L., Loret de Mola, C., & Victora, C. G. (2015). Breastfeeding and intelligence: A systematic review and meta-analysis. *Acta Paediatrica, 104* (S467), 14–9. https://doi.org/10.1111/apa.13139.

Horwood, C., Surie, A., Haskins, L. et al. (2020). Attitudes and perceptions about breastfeeding among female and male informal workers in India and South Africa. *BMC Public Health, 20*(1), 875. https://doi.org/10.1186/s12889-020-09013-9.

Hughes, O., Mohamad, M. M., Doyle, P., & Burke, G. (2018). The significance of breastfeeding on sleep patterns during the first 48 hours postpartum for first time mothers. *Journal of Obstetrics and Gynaecology, 38*(3), 316–20. https://doi.org/10.1080/01443615.2017.1353594.

Hurtado, A. M., Hill, K., Hurtado, I., & Kaplan, H. (1992). Trade-Offs between female food acquisition and child care among hiwi and ache foragers. *Human Nature, 3*(3), 185–216. https://doi.org/10.1007/BF02692239.

Jamison, A. M., Quinn, S. C., & Freimuth, V. S. (2019). 'You don't trust a government vaccine': Narratives of institutional trust and influenza vaccin-ation among African American and white adults. *Social Science & Medicine, 221*, 87–94. https://doi.org/10.1016/j.socscimed.2018.12.020.

Jelliffe, D. B., & Jelliffe, E. P. (1977). 'Breast is best': Modern meanings. *New England Journal of Medicine, 297*(17), 912–5.

Jolly, K., Ingram, L., Khan, K. S. et al. (2012). Systematic review of peer support for breastfeeding continuation: Metaregression analysis of the effect of setting, intensity, and timing. *BMJ, 344*, d8287. https://doi.org/10.1136/bmj.d8287.

Joseph, S. C. (1981). The anatomy of the infant formula controversy. *American Journal of Diseases of Children, 135*(10), 889–92.

Kikuchi, S., Nishihara, K., Horiuchi, S., & Eto, H. (2020). The influence of feeding method on a mother's circadian rhythm and on the development of her infant's circadian rest-activity rhythm. *Early Human Development, 145*, 105046. https://doi.org/10.1016/j.earlhumdev.2020.105046.

Kramer, M. S., Chalmers, B., Hodnett, E. D. et al. (2001). Promotion of breastfeeding intervention trial (PROBIT) A randomized trial in the republic of belarus. *JAMA, 285*(4), 413–20. https://doi.org/10.1001/jama.285.4.413.

Larsen, J. S., Hall, E. O. C., & Aagaard, H. (2008). Shattered expectations: When mothers' confidence in breastfeeding is undermined – a metasynthesis. *Scandinavian Journal of Caring Sciences, 22*(4), 653–61. https://doi.org/10.1111/j.1471-6712.2007.00572.x.

Laurent, C. (2003). Baby milk company fined for advertising direct to consumers. *BMJ, 327*(7410), 307. https://doi.org/10.1136/bmj.327.7410.307.

Lefèvre, C. M., Sharp, J. A., & Nicholas, K. R. (2010). Evolution of lactation: Ancient origin and extreme adaptations of the lactation system. *Annual Review of Genomics and Human Genetics, 11*(1), 219–38. https://doi.org/10.1146/annurev-genom-082509-141806.

Legesse, M., Demena, M., Mesfin, F., & Haile, D. (2015). Factors associated with colostrum avoidance among mothers of children aged less than 24 months in Raya Kobo district, North-eastern Ethiopia: Community-based cross-sectional study. *Journal of Tropical Pediatrics, 61*(5), 357–63. https://doi.org/10.1093/tropej/fmv039.

Lonsdorf, E. V., Stanton, M. A., Pusey, A. E., & Murray, C. M. (2020). Sources of variation in weaned age among wild chimpanzees in Gombe National Park, Tanzania. *American Journal of Physical Anthropology, 171*(3), 419–29. https://doi.org/10.1002/ajpa.23986.

Lowe, P. (2016). *Reproductive health and maternal sacrifice*. Springer.

Lutter, C. K., & Morrow, A. L. (2013). Protection, promotion, and support and global trends in breastfeeding. *Advances in Nutrition, 4*(2), 213–9. https://doi.org/10.3945/an.112.003111.

Marmot, M. (2005). Social determinants of health inequalities. *The Lancet, 365*(9464), 1099–104. https://doi.org/10.1016/S0140-6736(05)71146-6.

Marmot, M., & Allen, J. J. (2014). Social determinants of health equity. *American Journal of Public Health, 104*(S4), S517–S519. https://doi.org/10.2105/AJPH.2014.302200.

Martin, M. (2017). Mixed-feeding in humans: Evolution and current implications. In *Breastfeeding* (pp. 140–54). Routledge.

Martucci, J., & Barnhill, A. (2018). Examining the use of 'natural' in breastfeeding promotion: Ethical and practical concerns. *Journal of Medical Ethics, 44*(9), 615. https://doi.org/10.1136/medethics-2017-104455.

Matanda, D. J., Mittelmark, M. B., & Kigaru, D. M. D. (2014). Breast-, complementary and bottle-feeding practices in Kenya: Stagnant trends were experienced from 1998 to 2009. *Nutrition Research, 34*(6), 507–17. https://doi.org/10.1016/j.nutres.2014.05.004.

Maternity Action. (2022, March). *Breastfeeding while out and about*. https://maternityaction.org.uk/advice/breastfeeding-in-public-places/.

McAndrew, F., Thompson, J., Fellows, L. et al. (2012). Infant feeding survey 2010. *Leeds: Health and Social Care Information Centre, 2*(1).

McFadden, A., Gavine, A., Renfrew, M. et al. (2017). Support for healthy breastfeeding mothers with healthy term babies. *Cochrane Database of Systematic Reviews, 2.* https://doi.org/10.1002/14651858.CD001141.pub5

McGuire, E. (2019). Insufficient glandular tissue: A case report. *Breastfeeding Review, 27*(3), 53–9. https://search.informit.org/doi/10.3316/ielapa .869289712459730.

McLeish, J., Harvey, M., Redshaw, M., & Alderdice, F. (2021). A qualitative study of first time mothers' experiences of postnatal social support from health professionals in England. *Women and Birth, 34*(5), e451–e460. https://doi.org/10.1016/j.wombi.2020.10.012.

McLeroy, K. R., Bibeau, D., Steckler, A., & Glanz, K. (1988). An ecological perspective on health promotion programs. *Health Education Quarterly, 15* (4), 351–77. https://doi.org/10.1177/109019818801500401.

Michaelsen, K., Skafte, L., Badsberg, J., & Jørgensen, M. (1990). Variation in macronutrients in human bank milk: Influencing factors and implications for human milk banking. *Journal of Pediatric Gastroenterology and Nutrition, 11*(2), 229–39. https://doi.org/10.1097/00005176-199008000-00013.

Morgan, T., & Laland, K. (2012). The biological bases of conformity. *Frontiers in Neuroscience, 6.* www.frontiersin.org/articles/10.3389/fnins.2012.00087.

Morris, C., Zaraté de la Fuente, G. A., Williams, C. E. T., & Hirst, C. (2016). UK views toward breastfeeding in public: An analysis of the public's response to the claridge's incident. *Journal of Human Lactation, 32*(3), 472–80. https:// doi.org/10.1177/0890334416648934.

Morrison, A. H., Gentry, R., & Anderson, J. (2019). Mothers' reasons for early breastfeeding cessation. *MCN: The American Journal of Maternal/Child Nursing, 44*(6). https://journals.lww.com/mcnjournal/Fulltext/2019/11000/ Mothers__Reasons_for_Early_Breastfeeding_Cessation.4.aspx.

Myers, S., Page, A. E., & Emmott, E. H. (2021). The differential role of practical and emotional support in infant feeding experience in the UK. *Philosophical Transactions of the Royal Society B: Biological Sciences, 376*(1827), 20200034. https://doi.org/10.1098/rstb.2020.0034.

Navarro-Rosenblatt, D., & Garmendia, M.-L. (2018). Maternity leave and its impact on breastfeeding: A review of the literature. *Breastfeeding Medicine, 13*(9), 589–97. https://doi.org/10.1089/bfm.2018.0132.

Negrey, J. D., Emery Thompson, M., Dunn, C. D. et al. (2022). Female reproduction and viral infection in a long-lived mammal. *Journal of Animal Ecology.* https://doi.org/10.1111/1365-2656.13799.

Neifert, M. R. (2001). Prevention of breastfeeding tragedies. *Pediatric Clinics*, *48*(2), 273–97. https://doi.org/10.1016/s0031-3955(08)70026-9.

Nguyen, T. T., Alayón, S., Jimerson, A. et al. (2017). The association of a large-scale television campaign with exclusive breastfeeding prevalence in vietnam. *American Journal of Public Health*, *107*(2), 312–8. https://doi.org/10.2105/AJPH.2016.303561.

Nguyen, P. H., Keithly, S. C., Nguyen, N. T. et al. (2013). Prelacteal feeding practices in Vietnam: Challenges and associated factors. *BMC Public Health*, *13*(1), 932. https://doi.org/10.1186/1471-2458-13-932.

Noonan, M. (2011). Breastfeeding: Is my baby getting enough milk? *British Journal of Midwifery*, *19*(2), 82–9. https://doi.org/10.12968/bjom.2011.19.2.82.

Norholt, H. (2020). Revisiting the roots of attachment: A review of the biological and psychological effects of maternal skin-to-skin contact and carrying of full-term infants. *Infant Behavior and Development*, *60*, 101441. https://doi.org/10.1016/j.infbeh.2020.101441.

Nuffield Trust. (31 March 2022). *What proportion of mothers in England start and continue to breastfeed?* www.nuffieldtrust.org.uk/chart/what-proportion-of-mothers-in-england-start-and-continue-to-breastfeed-4.

Office for Health Improvement and Disparities. (2021). *Breastfeeding at 6 to 8 weeks after birth: Annual data 2020 to 2021*. www.gov.uk/government/statistics/breastfeeding-at-6-to-8-weeks-after-birth-annual-data-2020-to-2021.

Ogbo, F. A., Akombi, B. J., Ahmed, K. Y. et al. (2020). Breastfeeding in the community – How can partners/fathers help? A systematic review. *International Journal of Environmental Research and Public Health*, *17*(2). https://doi.org/10.3390/ijerph17020413

Page, A. E., Emmott, E. H., & Myers, S. (2022). Testing the buffering hypothesis: Breastfeeding problems, cessation, and social support in the UK. *American Journal of Human Biology*, *34*(2), e23621. https://doi.org/10.1002/ajhb.23621.

Palmer, G. (2009). *The politics of breastfeeding: When breasts are bad for business* (3rd updated and rev. ed.). Pinter & Martin.

Parry, K., Taylor, E., Hall-Dardess, P., Walker, M., & Labbok, M. (2013). Understanding Women's Interpretations of Infant Formula Advertising. *Birth*, *40*(2), 115–24. https://doi.org/10.1111/birt.12044.

Pereira-Kotze, C., Doherty, T., & Swart, E. C. (2020). Use of social media platforms by manufacturers to market breast-milk substitutes in South Africa. *BMJ Global Health*, *5*(12), e003574. https://doi.org/10.1136/bmjgh-2020-003574.

Pérez-Escamilla, R., Martinez, J. L., & Segura-Pérez, S. (2016). Impact of the Baby-friendly Hospital Initiative on breastfeeding and child health outcomes: A systematic review. *Maternal & Child Nutrition, 12*(3), 402–17. https://doi.org/10.1111/mcn.12294.

Picard, C., Fioramonti, J., Francois, A. et al. (2005). Review article: Bifidobacteria as probiotic agents – physiological effects and clinical benefits. *Alimentary Pharmacology & Therapeutics, 22*(6), 495–512. https://doi.org/10.1111/j.1365-2036.2005.02615.x.

Public Health England. (2021). *Early years high impact area 3: Supporting breastfeeding.* GOV.UK. www.gov.uk/government/publications/commissioning-of-public-health-services-for-children/early-years-high-impact-area-3-supporting-breastfeeding.

Quigley, K. M., Moore, G. A., Propper, C. B., Goldman, B. D., & Cox, M. J. (2017). Vagal regulation in breastfeeding infants and their mothers. *Child Development, 88*(3), 919–33. https://doi.org/10.1111/cdev.12641.

Quigley, M. A., Kelly, Y. J., & Sacker, A. (2007). Breastfeeding and hospitalization for diarrheal and respiratory infection in the United Kingdom millennium cohort study. *Pediatrics, 119*(4), e837–e842. https://doi.org/10.1542/peds.2006-2256.

Quinlan, R. J., & Quinlan, M. B. (2008). Human lactation, pair-bonds, and alloparents. *Human Nature, 19*(1), 87–102. https://doi.org/10.1007/s12110-007-9026-9.

Raju, T. N. K. (2011). Breastfeeding is a dynamic biological process –not simply a meal at the breast. *Breastfeeding Medicine, 6*(5), 257–9. https://doi.org/10.1089/bfm.2011.0081.

Ramani, S., Shaikh, N., Das, S. et al. (2019). 'Everybody breastfeeds if they have milk': Factors that shape exclusive breastfeeding practices in informal settlements of Mumbai, India. *International Breastfeeding Journal, 14*(1), 10. https://doi.org/10.1186/s13006-019-0204-2.

Rempel, L. A., Rempel, J. K., & Moore, K. C. J. (2017). Relationships between types of father breastfeeding support and breastfeeding outcomes. *Maternal & Child Nutrition, 13*(3), e12337. https://doi.org/10.1111/mcn.12337.

Rendell, L., Fogarty, L., Hoppitt, W. J. E. et al. (2011). Cognitive culture: Theoretical and empirical insights into social learning strategies. *Trends in Cognitive Sciences, 15*(2), 68–76. https://doi.org/10.1016/j.tics.2010.12.002.

Renfrew, M. J., Pokhrel, S., Quigley, M. et al. (2012). *Preventing disease and saving resources: The potential contribution of increasing breastfeeding rates in the UK.* UNICEF UK. www.unicef.org.uk/wp-content/uploads/sites/2/2012/11/Preventing_disease_saving_resources.pdf.

Roberts, T. J., Carnahan, E., & Gakidou, E. (2013). Can breastfeeding promote child health equity? A comprehensive analysis of breastfeeding patterns across the developing world and what we can learn from them. *BMC Medicine*, *11*(1), 254. https://doi.org/10.1186/1741-7015-11-254.

Robinson, K. H. (2013). *Innocence, knowledge and the construction of childhood: The contradictory nature of sexuality and censorship in children's contemporary lives*. Routledge.

Rudzik, A. E. F., & Ball, H. L. (2021). Biologically normal sleep in the mother-infant dyad. *American Journal of Human Biology*, *33*(5), e23589. https://doi.org/10.1002/ajhb.23589.

Rudzik, A. E. F., Robinson-Smith, L., & Ball, H. L. (2018). Discrepancies in maternal reports of infant sleep vs. Actigraphy by mode of feeding. *Sleep Medicine*, *49*, 90–8. https://doi.org/10.1016/j.sleep.2018.06.010.

Scelza, B. A., & Hinde, K. (2019). Crucial contributions: A biocultural study of grandmothering during the perinatal period. *Human Nature*, *30*(4), 371–97. https://doi.org/10.1007/s12110-019-09356-2.

Scott, J. A., & Mostyn, T. (2003). Women's experiences of breastfeeding in a bottle-feeding culture. *Journal of Human Lactation*, *19*(3), 270–277. https://doi.org/10.1177/0890334403255225.

Sear, R. (2021). The male breadwinner nuclear family is not the 'traditional' human family, and promotion of this myth may have adverse health consequences. *Philosophical Transactions of the Royal Society B: Biological Sciences*, *376*(1827), 20200020. https://doi.org/10.1098/rstb.2020.0020.

Sellen, D. W. (2007). Evolution of infant and young child feeding: Implications for contemporary public health. *Annual Review of Nutrition*, *27*(1), 123–48. https://doi.org/10.1146/annurev.nutr.25.050304.092557.

Simpson, D. A., Carson, C., Kurinczuk, J. J., & Quigley, M. A. (2022). Trends and inequalities in breastfeeding continuation from 1 to 6 weeks: Findings from six population-based British cohorts, 1985–2010. *European Journal of Clinical Nutrition*, *76*(5), 671–9. https://doi.org/10.1038/s41430-021-01031-z.

Smith, T. M., Austin, C., Hinde, K., Vogel, E. R., & Arora, M. (2017). Cyclical nursing patterns in wild orangutans. *Science Advances*, *3*(5), e1601517. https://doi.org/10.1126/sciadv.1601517.

Spatz, D. L. (2020). Using gender-neutral terms in lactation. *MCN: The American Journal of Maternal/Child Nursing*, *45*(1), 61–61. https://doi.org/10.1097/NMC .0000000000000594.

Srimoragot, M., Hershberger, P. E., Park, C., Hernandez, T. L., & Izci Balserak, B. (2022). Infant feeding type and maternal sleep during the postpartum period: A systematic review and meta-analysis. *Journal of Sleep Research*, e13625. https://doi.org/10.1111/jsr.13625.

Standish, K. R., & Parker, M. G. (2022). Social determinants of breastfeeding in the United States. *Clinical Therapeutics*, *44*(2), 186–92. https://doi.org/10.1016/j.clinthera.2021.11.010.

Stuebe, A. M., & Chen, M. J. (2022). 21 – Reproductive function during lactation. In R. A. Lawrence & R. M. Lawrence (eds.), *Breastfeeding (Ninth Edition)* (pp. 651–61). Elsevier. https://doi.org/10.1016/B978-0-323-68013-4.00021-3.

Swanson, V., Power, K., Kaur, B., Carter, H., & Shepherd, K. (2006). The impact of knowledge and social influences on adolescents' breast-feeding beliefs and intentions. *Public Health Nutrition*, *9*(3), 297–305. https://doi.org/10.1079/PHN2005845.

Taylor, A. M., Teijlingen, E. van, Ryan, K. M., & Alexander, J. (2019). 'Scrutinised, judged and sabotaged': A qualitative video diary study of first-time breastfeeding mothers. *Midwifery*, *75*, 16–23. https://doi.org/10.1016/j.midw.2019.04.004.

Theurich, M. A., Davanzo, R., Busck-Rasmussen, M. et al. (2019). Breastfeeding rates and programs in Europe: A survey of 11 national breast-feeding committees and representatives. *Journal of Pediatric Gastroenterology and Nutrition*, *68*(3), 400–7. https://doi.org/10.1097/mpg.0000000000002234.

Thomson, P., Medina, D. A., & Garrido, D. (2018). Human milk oligosaccharides and infant gut bifidobacteria: Molecular strategies for their utilization. *Food Microbiology*, *75*, 37–46. https://doi.org/10.1016/j.fm.2017.09.001.

Trickey, H., & Ashmore, S. (2017). Infant feeding: Changing the conversation. *Infant*, *13*(1), 26–8. www.infantjournal.co.uk/pdf/inf_073_ngi.pdf.

Tschiderer, L., Seekircher, L., Kunutsor, S. K. et al. (2022). Breastfeeding is associated with a reduced maternal cardiovascular risk: Systematic review and meta-analysis involving data from 8 studies and 1 192 700 parous women. *Journal of the American Heart Association*, *11*(2), e022746. https://doi.org/10.1161/JAHA.121.022746

Tully, K. P., & Ball, H. L. (2013). Trade-offs underlying maternal breastfeeding decisions: A conceptual model. *Maternal & Child Nutrition*, *9*(1), 90–98. https://doi.org/10.1111/j.1740-8709.2011.00378.x

UNICEF. (2006). *1990-2005 Celebrating the innocenti declaration on the protection, promotion and support of breastfeeding: Past achievements, present challenges and priority actions for infant and young child feeding.* www.unicef-irc.org/publications/pdf/celebrating_2nded.pdf.

UNICEF. (2016). *From the first hour of life: Making the case for improved infant and young child feeding everywhere.* www.unicef.org/media/49801/file/From-the-first-hour-of-life-ENG.pdf.

UNICEF UK. (2017). *Baby friendly initiative: Call to action.* www .youtube.com/watch?v=7yNvkk_LfpU.

UNICEF UK. (2022a). *About the baby friendly initiative.* www.unicef.org.uk/baby friendly/about/

UNICEF UK. (2022b). *Breastfeeding in the UK.* www.unicef.org.uk/baby friendly/about/breastfeeding-in-the-uk/.

Uvnäs-Moberg, K., Ekström-Bergström, A., Buckley, S. et al. (2020). Maternal plasma levels of oxytocin during breastfeeding – A systematic review. *PLOS ONE, 15*(8), e0235806. https://doi.org/10.1371/journal.pone.0235806.

Victora, C. G., Bahl, R., Barros, A. J. D. et al. (2016). Breastfeeding in the 21st century: Epidemiology, mechanisms, and lifelong effect. *The Lancet, 387* (10017), 475–490. https://doi.org/10.1016/S0140-6736(15)01024-7.

Waits, A., Guo, C.-Y., & Chien, L.-Y. (2018). Evaluation of factors contributing to the decline in exclusive breastfeeding at 6 months postpartum: The 2011-2016 National Surveys in Taiwan. *Birth, 45*(2), 184–92. https://doi .org/10.1111/birt.12340.

Walks, M. (2017). Chestfeeding as gender fluid practice. In C. Tomori, A. E. L. Palmquist, E. A. Quinn (Eds.), *Breastfeeding: New anthropological approaches* (pp. 155–69). Routledge.

Walters, D. D., Phan, L. T. H., & Mathisen, R. (2019). The cost of not breastfeeding: Global results from a new tool. *Health Policy and Planning, 34*(6), 407–17. https://doi.org/10.1093/heapol/czz050.

Wells, J. (2006). The role of cultural factors in human breastfeeding: Adaptive behaviour or biopower. *Journal of Human Ecology, 14*, 39–47.

Wells, J. C. K., Nesse, R. M., Sear, R., Johnstone, R. A., & Stearns, S. C. (2017). Evolutionary public health: Introducing the concept. *The Lancet, 390* (10093), 500–9. https://doi.org/10.1016/S0140-6736(17)30572-X.

WHO. (2008). *Social determinants of health.* WHO Regional Office for South-East Asia.

WHO. (2014). *Comprehensive implementation plan on maternal, infant and young child nutrition.* http://apps.who.int/iris/bitstream/handle/10665/113048/ WHO_NMH_NHD_14.1_eng.pdf;jsessionid=AD784AB0E3552127 F4F2E95263166C86?sequence=1.

WHO. (2017a). *Guidance on ending the inappropriate promotion of foods for infants and young children: Implementation manual.* www.who.int/publica tions/i/item/9789241513470.

WHO. (2017b). *Guideline: Protecting, promoting and supporting breastfeeding in facilities providing maternity and newborn services.* www.who.int/publica tions/i/item/9789241550086.

WHO. (2018). *Guideline: Counselling of women to improve breastfeeding practices*. World Health Organisation. www.who.int/publications/i/item/9789241550468.

WHO & UNICEF. (2018). *Implementation guidance: Protecting, promoting and supporting breastfeeding in facilities providing maternity and newborn services: The revised baby-friendly hospital initiative.* https://apps.who.int/iris/handle/10665/272943.

WHO Collaborative Study Team. (2000). Effect of breastfeeding on infant and child mortality due to infectious diseases in less developed countries: A pooled analysis. *The Lancet, 355*(9202), 451–5. https://doi.org/10.1016/S0140-6736(00)82011-5.

Williams, H. (2006). And not a drop to drink' – Why water is harmful for newborns. *Breastfeeding Review, 14*(2), 5–9.

Williamson, I., Leeming, D., Lyttle, S., & Johnson, S. (2012). 'It should be the most natural thing in the world': Exploring first-time mothers' breastfeeding difficulties in the UK using audio-diaries and interviews. *Maternal & Child Nutrition, 8*(4), 434–47. https://doi.org/10.1111/j.1740-8709.2011.00328.x.

Cambridge Elements $^{\equiv}$

Applied Evolutionary Science

David F. Bjorklund
Florida Atlantic University
David F. Bjorklund is a Professor of Psychology at Florida Atlantic University in Boca Raton, Florida. He is the Editor-in-Chief of the *Journal of Experimental Child Psychology*, the Vice President of the Evolution Institute, and has written numerous articles and books on evolutionary developmental psychology, with a particular interest in the role of immaturity in evolution and development.

Editorial Board

About the Series
This series presents original, concise, and authoritative reviews of key topics in applied evolutionary science. Highlighting how an evolutionary approach can be applied to real-world social issues, many Elements in this series will include findings from programs that have produced positive educational, social, economic, or behavioral benefits. Cambridge Elements in Applied Evolutionary Science is published in association with the Evolution Institute.

Printed in the United States
by Baker & Taylor Publisher Services